From Eccles Cake to Hawkshead Wig

A Celebration of Northern Food

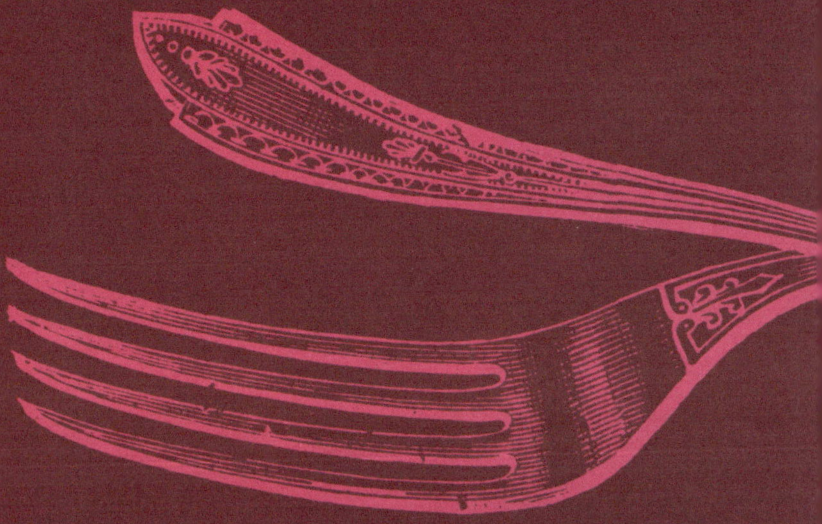

From Eccles Cake to Hawkshead Wig

A Celebration of Northern Food

Laura Mason and Catherine Brown

Foreword by Hugh Fearnley-Whittingstall

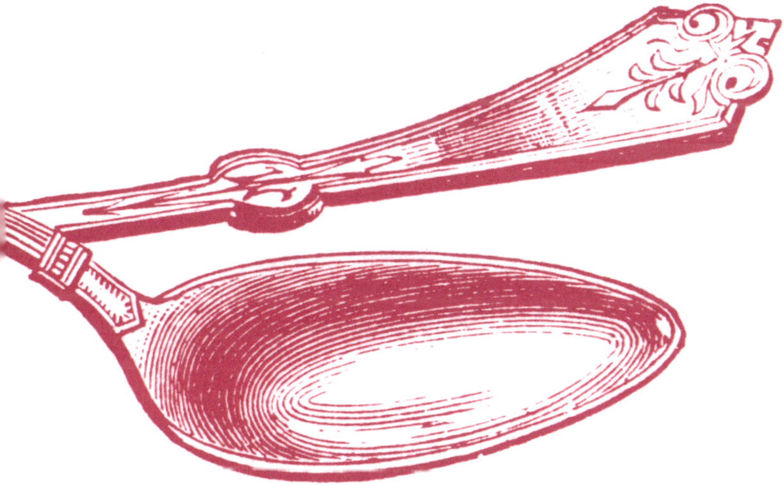

Harper Press

An imprint of HarperCollins*Publishers*

Harper*Press*
An imprint of HarperCollins*Publishers*
77–85 Fulham Palace Road
Hammersmith, London W6 8JB
www.harpercollins.co.uk

Published by Harper Press in 2007

First published in Great Britain in 1999
as part of *Traditional Foods of Britain*
by Prospect Books
Allaleigh House, Blackawton, Totnes, Devon TQ9 7DL

Subsequently published by Harper*Press* in 2006 as part of *The Taste of Britain*
Original design by 'OMEDESIGN

9 8 7 6 5 4 3 2 1

A catalogue record for this book
is available from the British Library

ISBN: 978-0-00-726788-0

Design by Envy Design Ltd

Printed and bound in China

From Eccles Cakes to Hawkshead Wig is part of a series of books about regional British food which include:

From Bath Chaps to Bara Brith
The Taste of South West Britain

Bedfordshire Clangers and Lardy Cake
Traditional Foods from the South and South East

From Norfolk Knobs to Fidget Pie
Foods from the Heart of England and East Anglia

From Petticoat Tails to Arbroath Smokies
Traditional Foods of Scotland

These books originally formed part of the complete volume, *The Taste of Britain*, published by Harper*Press* in 2006.

Contents

Foreword

Much is made these days of British food culture. Chefs and food writers, myself included, are keen to tell you that it's thriving, it should be celebrated, it's as good as anything our Continental cousins enjoy. Yet sometimes it seems as if our words come rolling back to us, as if bouncing off some distant landmass, unheard and unheeded along the way, so that we begin to have trouble persuading ourselves, let alone others, that there is something here worth fighting for.

The fact is that if you spend much time in supermarkets, or amongst the proliferation of branded fast foods on any high street, or if you eat in any but a handful of UK restaurants or pubs, then the concept of regional British food can seem a bit like Father Christmas, or Nirvana. A lovely romantic idea, but it doesn't really exist, does it?

Well, yes, it does. And if you're having trouble finding it, it may just be because you are looking in the wrong place. The problem, in part at least, is that the best, most uplifting stories about British food culture are being drowned out by the cacophony of mediocrity, and worse. The Turkey Twizzler is front page news – and rightly so, when it is making pre-basted, additive-laced butterballs of our children themselves. Shavings of Turkey 'ham' – 98 per cent fat free, of course – are filling the sandwiches of figure-conscious office workers the length and breadth of the nation. But the Norfolk Black, a real turkey slow-grown and bred for flavour, is out there, too – waiting to show you what he's worth. He's not making a song and dance – just gobbling quietly to himself. Track him down, and you're in for a revelation.

That's why this series of books are so timely, so necessary – and so brilliantly useful. They are a map, an investigative tool that will enable you to leave behind the homogenous and the bland, and set off on an exciting journey to find Britain's edible treasure – some of which may turn out to be hidden on your very doorstep.

I urge you not merely to browse them, but to use them. Because if you can get out there and discover for yourself some of our great British specialities – whether it's traditional sage Derby cheese, or the Yorkshire teacakes known as Fat Rascals, or a properly aged Suffolk cider vinegar – then you will discover, or at least remind yourself, that food can be so much more than fuel. That it can, several times a day, every day of our lives, relax us, stimulate us, and give us pleasure.

The foods described in this book can all work that small daily miracle of exciting our passions. Not all of them, for all of us. But each of them for some of us. They have been made and honed over generations – sometimes centuries – and they are still with us because enough of us – sometimes only just enough of us – love them. Of course, in many instances, we have yet to discover whether we love them or not. And that is why this book is so loaded with fantastic potential. Everybody has a new favourite food waiting for them in the pages ahead.

I've travelled fairly widely, if somewhat randomly, around Britain, and tracking down and tasting local foods has become an increasing priority for me. Very uplifting it is, too. Approach our regional food culture with a true sense of curiosity, and you can never become an old hand, or a jaded palate. I still feel a great sense of excitement and discovery when I finally get to eat a classic local dish on its own home turf. You can't easily deconstruct the magic formula of a well-made Lancashire Hot Pot, or a Dorset apple cake. It is in the nature of such dishes that their sum is greater than their parts. But you can, when you find a version that hits the spot, instantly appreciate how such dishes have survived the harsh natural selection of public taste, and come to delight, comfort and sustain families and groups of friends for so long.

Recently, for instance, I managed to track down my very first proper Yorkshire curd tart, its delectable filling made from colostrum – the very rich milk produced by a cow for her newborn calf. It was baked for me by a farmer's wife at home in her own kitchen, using the method passed down to her through her family, and it was wonderful – very rich, curdy and slightly crumbly – having a hint of cakiness without the flouriness (I told you deconstruction was a vain enterprise). Anyway, it was a world away from any 'regular' custard tart I'd tried before. What I learnt from that experience, and from many similar ones, is that regionality really does matter. If that tart had been made in Dorset or in the Highlands, it wouldn't have tasted the same. And if it had not been made at all, the world – and on that drizzly autumn day, me – would have been the poorer for it.

There are so many factors that affect the way a food turns out. Cheese is the best example. I love cheese – 'milk's leap toward immortality' as someone once said – and it never ceases to amaze me. It's made from milk, of course, plus something that will make the milk curdle (usually rennet, but sometimes quirkier coagulants, like nettle juice). Two basic ingredients. Yet cheese is one of the most diverse foods known to man. There are hundreds of varieties in the British Isles alone – and a bowlful of fresh, pillowy Scottish crowdie differs so greatly from a nutty Somerset cheddar that it's hard to believe they're basically the same stuff. The breed of cattle and their diet, the local water and pasture, the yeasts and bacteria that live locally in the air, the techniques used to curdle the milk, the way the cheese is pressed, turned, and aged – all these things affect the outcome.

That's why it seems absolutely right to me that only cheese made in a handful of Midlands dairies can be called Stilton, and that beer brewed with the gypsum-rich water in Burton-upon-Trent is labelled as such. What's more, if you understand why regional products are unique – that it's high temperatures and seaweed fertiliser that make Jersey Royals taste different to any other potatoes, for instance – then you know more about food in general. An understanding of regional diversity can only make us more intelligent and appreciative eaters.

This understanding is not always easy to come by. Most other European countries have long taken for granted that local foods should be protected, their unique identity preserved. Hence the French

AOC and the Italian DOC systems. But it's an idea not everyone in this country is comfortable with. I put this down to two things, and the first is the creeping curse of supermarket culture. The big multiple retailers try to tell us that we can eat whatever we want, whenever we want and indeed wherever we want. If you understand the seasonal nature of fresh produce, you know this is neither true nor desirable – and the same goes for regionality. You might not be able to buy genuine Arbroath smokies in every shop in the land, but that is precisely what makes them special when you do find them.

The second reason for resistance to regional labelling is illustrated by the pork pie issue. The pie makers of Melton Mowbray are currently battling to have their product awarded PGI (Protected Geographic Indication) status. That would mean only pies made in the area, to a traditional recipe, could carry the name. Other pork pie makers, from other areas, object to this. They want to call their products Melton Mowbray pies, too, arguing that their recipe is much the same. That's nonsense, of course: a recipe is only the beginning of a dish, a mere framework. The where, the how and the who of its making are just as important. But why would you even want to call your pie a Mowbray pie if it comes from London, or Swansea? Only, perhaps, if you know the real Mowbray pies taste better, and you can't be bothered to make your own recipe good enough to compete.

All of which goes to show why the issue of regionality is as relevant today as it ever has been. It's important not to see *From Eccles Cake to Hawkshead Wig* as a history book, a compendium of nostalgic culinary whimsy. The food included here is alive and well, and there is nothing described in these pages that you can't eat today, as long as you go to the right place. That's perhaps the most important criterion for inclusion because our regional food traditions are just as much part of the future as the past. At least, they had better be, or we will be in serious trouble.

The implications for our health, and the health of our environment, are far-reaching. If we eat, say, fruit that's produced locally, not only do we reduce the food miles that are wrecking our climate, but that fruit will be fresher and richer in nutrients. If we can go to a butcher's shop to buy meat that's been raised nearby, we can ask the butcher how it was farmed, and how it was slaughtered. And perhaps we can take our children with us, so they learn something too. In the end, a local food culture, supplied in the main by contiguous communities, militates against secrecy, adulteration – cruelty even – and in favour of transparency, accountability and good practice. What could be more reassuring than knowing the names and addresses of the people who produce your food?

I don't think it's overstating the case, either, to say that a knowledge of regional cooking promotes resourcefulness and a renewed respect for food in all of us. Regional dishes are, by their very nature, simple things. This is folk cooking – a 'nose to tail' approach that uses whatever's available and makes it go as far as possible. For a while now – since conspicuous consumption has become practically an end in itself – our predecessors' abhorrence of throwing away anything may have seemed at best, quaint, at worst, laughable. But as we begin to come to terms with the consequences of our 'have it all now' culture, it is becoming clear that ethical production, good husbandry, environmental responsibility and kitchen thrift all go hand in hand. The frugal culture that gave birth to chitterlings and lardy cake, Bath chaps and bread pudding is something we should be proud to belong to. To re-embrace it can only do us good.

Aside from their currency, the foods in this book have had to prove themselves in other ways. They must be unique to a specific region and they must have longevity, having been made or produced for at least 75 years. Finally, they must be, to use a rather ugly word, 'artisanal'. That means that special knowledge and skills are required to make them properly. Which brings me to one crucial element of good food that should never be forgotten: the people who make it. Almost without exception, the brewers, bakers, cooks, farmers and fishermen who produce traditional foods are what you might call 'characters'. This doesn't mean they are yokels caught in a yesteryear time warp. They are people of passion and commitment, intelligence and good humour, and often extraordinary specialist knowledge. And they know more than most of us about the meaning of life.

Not a single one of them goes to work in the morning in order to make lots of money – you certainly don't choose to devote your life to bannock-making in the hope it will furnish you with a swimming pool and a Ferrari. They do it because they believe in it and, ultimately, feel it is worthwhile. In their own quiet and industrious way, they understand just how much is at stake. The future of civilized, communal, respectful life on our islands? It is not preposterous to suggest it. Use your regular custom and generously expressed enthusiasm to support this modest army of dedicated souls, working away in their kitchens, gardens, orchards breweries and smokehouses all over Britain, and you do a great deal more than simply save a cheese, or a beer, for posterity. You help save the next generation from the tyranny of industrial mediocrity.

Amid this talk of pride and principles, it's crucial not to lose sight of the fact that this is food to be enjoyed, celebrated – and shared with friends. Dishes don't survive down the centuries unless they taste good. You may not need much persuasion to try some of the buttery cakes or fabulously fresh fruit and veg described in these pages. But you will perhaps need a sense of adventure to rediscover the charms of some of the entries. Be ready to cast your squeamishness aside and sample some tripe, some tongue, some trotters as well. If the experience of visitors to our River Cottage events here in Dorset is anything to go by, I'm betting you'll be pleasantly surprised. You'll be taking a pig's head home from the butcher's and making your own brawn before you can say, 'Er, not for me, thanks.'

One element of this series of books to be richly savoured is the language. They are written, by Laura Mason and Catherine Brown, without hyperbole, but with a precision and clarity that far better express their authors' underlying passion and purpose. Another thing that makes them a joy to read is their embrace of the regional food vernacular: Dorset knobs, Puggie Buns, Singin' Hinnnies, Black Bullets and Mendip Wallfish are all to be revelled in for their names alone. Indeed, some might be tempted to enjoy them chiefly as a glorious catalogue of eccentricity, a celebration of the cowsheel and the careless gooseberry, of the head cheese and the damson cheese (neither of which are actually cheese) that make British food so charming and idiosyncratic.

But to do so would be to miss out. Now that this book exists, now that it is in your hands, use it to bring about change. It should not be taken as a slice of the past, in aspic, but as a well-stocked store cupboard, with the potential to enrich our future food culture. See it not as a preservation order for British regional foods, but a call to action. Use this book as a guide, not merely to seek out delicious things that you've never tried before, but also to recreate some of them in your own kitchen. Do that and you'll be actively participating in a great food culture that has always been with us, that is often hidden beneath the mass-produced, homogenous, seasonless food we are so frequently offered, but which may yet have a vibrant future.

This book - along with the rest in the series - is a thorough and splendid answer to the question 'What is British food?' Use it well, and it may help to ensure that is still a meaningful question a hundred years from now.

Hugh Fearnley-Whittingstall

Preface

In 1994 we embarked on a mission to describe as many British foods with regional affiliations as we could find. We were part of a Europe-wide project working within a framework – handed down from Brussels – which demanded a link to the *terroir* (soil). In fact the project, named Euroterroir, was more suited to rural southern Europe than industrialized, urbanized Britain. How do you link Yorkshire Relish to the soil? But ultimately we succeeded in writing up some four hundred British entries. And along the way we asked some broader questions – what are our traditional foods? What is the character of British taste?

We've discovered that many rural treasures had survived against the odds. That sometimes foods with traditional or regional affiliations languished unloved. That sometimes British foods, though not always linking directly to the *terroir*, did have other powerful historical influences which made them special, and distinct, from the rest of Europe. No other country in Europe has a history of spicing to match the British.

Yet our homogenized food supply was clearly inflicting a far-reaching loss of local distinctiveness and quality. The idea, inherent in the project, that foods should be the property of a place and its community (*terroir*, in the context of food in France, carries implications of regionality, cultural groupings and the influence of trade and climate), rather than the trademarked possession of an individual or company, was especially alien.

Our initial research complete, we felt confident that either the Ministry of Agriculture or Food from Britain would take up the cause and publish a book based on the work which had taken us two years to complete. Instead, it was a small publisher in Devon (Tom Jaine of

Prospect Books) who kept the flag flying and *Traditional Foods of Britain* was published in 1999. Eight years on we welcome this new series published by HarperCollins.

We also welcome signs of change. Now, there is more awareness of commercial dilution, and dishonest imitation and therefore the need to protect food names, though the application process for producers is slow and difficult. There are certainly more small producers working locally, but they have to cope with numerous barriers. However much they protest otherwise, powerful supermarket central distribution systems and cut-throat pricing polices are not designed to foster local produce. And consumers do not always pause to consider the more subtle and elusive nuances of foods from closer to home.

Of course the ties of regionality do not suit foodstuffs, and in any case should be just one of many avenues open to British farmers and food producers. But it would be good to see more raw local ingredients transformed into distinctive foods since records show their rich variety in the past. Shops and markets bursting with colourful and varied local produce are one of the great pleasures of shopping for food on the continent. They exist because national policies and local custom support them. They should not be impossible in Britain. These books are not an end, but a beginning.

Laura Mason and Catherine Brown 2007

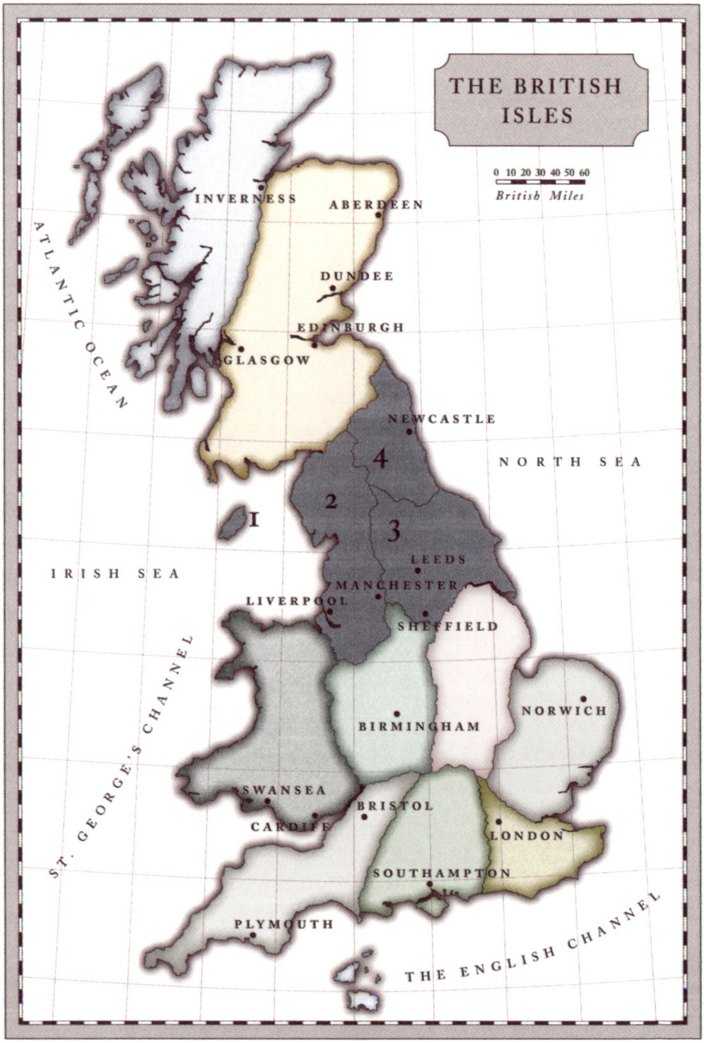
THE BRITISH ISLES
0 10 20 30 40 50 60
British Miles
INVERNESS
ABERDEEN
DUNDEE
EDINBURGH
GLASGOW
ATLANTIC OCEAN
NEWCASTLE
NORTH SEA
4
2
3
1
IRISH SEA
LEEDS
MANCHESTER
LIVERPOOL
SHEFFIELD
ST. GEORGE'S CHANNEL
NORWICH
BIRMINGHAM
SWANSEA
BRISTOL
CARDIFF
LONDON
SOUTHAMPTON
PLYMOUTH
THE ENGLISH CHANNEL

Regions

1. *Isle of Man*
2. *North West England*
3. *North England*
4. *North East England*

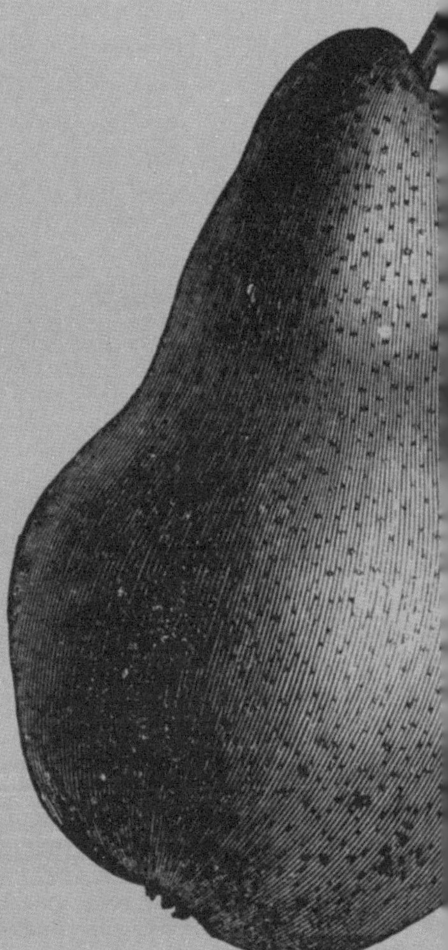

Isle of Man

Kipper (Manx)

DESCRIPTION:

Cold-smoked Manx kippers are about 22cm including head and tail, weighing approximately 120g. Colour: the skin is dark grey brown on the back, fading to silver on the belly, with a distinctly gold tinge; the flesh is dark golden brown. Flavour: mildly fishy, mellow, with salt more dominant than smoke; quite oily.

HISTORY:

The Isle of Man is a good base from which to catch herrings. There is an island tradition of salting and curing them to make either barrelled salt herring, or red herrings. These were much exported in the past. Kippered herring, made to the cure developed by John Woodger from Northumberland, first became popular in the 1840s and the process must have spread rapidly to other parts of the country. Certainly, it was well known by the time the company of George Devereaux was established in 1884. John Curtis, the other company producing Manx kippers, has also been in existence for about 100 years. Manx kippers are the traditional product. Isle of Man kippers, whilst made on the island, are not the same. They use dyes, illegal on Manx kippers.

TECHNIQUE:

The cure used for kippers on the Isle of Man is similar to that used elsewhere; the herring are prepared by splitting and cleaning; they are then brined for a short time, hung on tenter-hooks and smoked.

There are several points which make Manx kippers unique. Firstly, they are always undyed. Secondly, the excellence of the herring, which have a fat content and composition which render them highly suitable for this type of cure; fish caught early in the season – the Manx season is from June to August – are best, and those from Irish boats, which fish in pairs with 1 net between 2 boats, are preferred, as the fish landed by these are in excellent condition with no bruising. Finally, there is the skill and attention given to them during the smoking. Peter Canipa, who smokes fish for Devereaux and Son, uses a smoke temperature higher than that used elsewhere and remarks that timing is crucial to quality. This depends on the fishes' size and oil content and ambient temperature.

REGION OF PRODUCTION:

Isle of Man.

Scallop (Isle Of Man)

DESCRIPTION:

Great or king scallop (*Pecten maximus*): flat bottom shell and a concave upper shell; muscle diameter approximately 50mm; minimum legal carapace size 100mm. Queen scallop (*Chlamys opercularia*): top and bottom shells both concave; muscle diameter approximately 30mm. Princess scallop (an immature queen): muscle diameter approximately 10mm. The great scallop and the queen have beige shells, and a cream or white muscle surrounded by an orange roe. The princess scallop has a reddish-pink shell and a cream or white muscle but the roe, because of its age, has not developed. They have a distinctive and subtle sea-flavour from rich feeding in unpolluted northern waters.

HISTORY:

Dr Larch Garrad, of Manx National Heritage, observes that scallop shells have been found on the Isle of Man in archaeological deposits 2–3,000 years old, as well as in early medieval contexts. The extent to which they were used for food in the past is unknown, as they are difficult to fish without the aid of modern equipment. However, local people have a long-standing tradition of gathering food from the shore after storms, and certain pools are known for sometimes yielding scallops after high seas. The smaller queenies are also exposed at the ebb of very low spring tides and can be taken from boats. By the end of the nineteenth century, dredges from the Isle of Man capable of fishing scallops were being exhibited at international fishing exhibitions.

According to Dr A.R. Brand at the Port Erin Marine Laboratory, a fishery intended purely for scallops was founded on the Isle of Man in the 1930s. This rapidly became the most valuable fishery on the island and, with the exception of a few years in the 1970s when the herring yielded some excellent catches, has remained so.

An important dredged- and dived-scallop industry arose in the 1950s and 1960s, harvesting from natural West-coast beds. The scallops were exported to the British mainland and sold in Billingsgate. Research into scallop farming began on the Isle of Man in the early 1970s and, although no farming takes place there, the methods developed have been successfully applied off the West coast of Scotland, where the popularity of the farmed scallop has grown, partly due to its guarantee of quality. Scallops from natural beds can live for up to 20 years, when the texture of their muscle becomes tough.

TECHNIQUE:

In the wild, scallops spend most of their life on the sea bed and spawn many millions of eggs each year. These go through a free-swimming stage, during which time they are carried around on currents and tidal streams. After 3 or 4 weeks they settle on a suitable substrate such as seaweed. The muddy gravel sea bed round the Isle of Man provides suitable conditions and contains substantial natural scallop beds. The shellfish feed on phyto-plankton, and tidal currents provide some water movement, a necessity for scallops. They are harvested by dredging. The daily catch is processed on the island by shelling and cleaning; a small proportion is frozen, but most are exported, fresh and chilled, by air.

REGION OF PRODUCTION:

Isle of Man.

Manx Loghtan Sheep

DESCRIPTION:

DRESSED CARCASS WEIGHT FOR A 6-MONTH LOWLAND LAMB: ABOUT 18KG. THE LEAN MEAT IS DARK, CLOSE-GRAINED, WITH A VERY GOOD FLAVOUR.

HISTORY:

Manx Loghtans are visually arresting: they have a mouse brown coat (*loaghton* in Manx) and, whilst some are 2-horned, they are noted for the fact that many grow 4 horns. The latter characteristic is shared with Hebridean (St Kilda) sheep from Scotland, and Jacob's sheep, an ornamental parkland breed widely distributed in Britain. Manx Loghtans have close affinities with Icelandic and Scandinavian strains and may originate from stock brought to Britain by the Vikings (Hall & Clutton-Brock, 1989). For centuries they were the only sheep on the Isle of Man, providing both meat and wool. They went into decline with the arrival of improved breeds from the British mainland in the early nineteenth century.

Together with the other 4-horned and so-called primitive sheep, the Manx Loghtans really came to public attention in 1913 when a display was organized for an agricultural show by John Elwes. At this time, the breed was almost extinct, but a few people on the Isle of Man were sufficiently enthusiastic to conserve flocks. The formation of the Rare Breeds Survival Trust about 35 years ago led to a renewed interest. Several flocks were established on the mainland, and one was established on the Calf of Man, an almost uninhabited island at the southern end of the Isle, as a conservation measure against outbreak of disease amongst the main flocks.

TECHNIQUE:

The rolling hills of the Isle of Man are in a mild maritime climate with no great extremes of temperature, though very windy. The native flora is grass and heather, and the land generally well drained. The breed has developed to be hardy, grazing the unimproved grass of the higher land. It requires little or no supplementary feeding except before

lambing. The ewes are good mothers and prolific milkers. Lambs are raised outdoors with little human intervention. The breed is slow maturing and does not run to fat. As a meat sheep, there is some interest in crossing it with lowland terminal sires to give commercial lamb for the mass market. There is also interest in marketing it as a distinct breed, both on the Island and the mainland. However, in the past, there has been some prejudice against the sheep on the Isle of Man, which still works against effective marketing. Older people display an irrational distaste for the meat; abattoirs dislike the carcasses because they do not conform to official grading and, due to legislation from last century, butchers on the Isle of Man are not allowed to identify the meat as coming from Manx Loghtans. The breed society is working to overcome these problems and there is now some interest in the sheep as a local speciality.

PRODUCTION:

Some pure-bred Manx Loghtan meat reaches the market every year, but the quantity is not great, perhaps a few hundred lambs on the Isle of Man. Since the inauguration of a pedigree registration scheme, numbers have started to recover, and there are a few large flocks kept on the Isle of Man, including 3 owned by the Manx Museum. About 80 breeders in mainland Britain keep examples of the sheep.

REGION OF PRODUCTION:

ISLE OF MAN.

North West England

Damson

DESCRIPTION:

Dimensions: 3cm long. Weight: 6–8g. Form: small tear-shaped fruit. Colour: purple-black skin with powder blue bloom, yellow-green flesh. Flavour: sweet-sharp, aromatic.

HISTORY:

The name damson indicates the fruit of *Prunus institia*, native to Britain (Roach, 1985). The tree occurs in a wild form known as the bullace; the cultivated form, or damson, may have taken its name from Damascus, in Syria. There are English literary references to damsons from the fifteenth century onwards; they have always been popular in this country.

They are valued in the West Midlands and the North West. In both they were grown partly as a fruit crop and partly for use as a dye in the woollen industry. In the North West, the southern Lake District, especially the Lythe Valley, contains many old orchards of the trees. They were first planted here in large numbers in the 1850s. For a while they flourished, and much of the crop was sent to the cloth-weaving towns of Yorkshire, but picking became un-economic, and the orchards were neglected or grubbed up. A few were replanted in the 1950s.

The *Catalogue of Plums at the National Fruit Trials* (1978) records that a variety of damson known as Blue Violet, local to Westmoreland, was received in 1932. Westmoreland Damson is also a local name for another variety, more widespread in Britain, the prune damson, itself recorded at the Trials in 1950. Damsons from the southern Lake

District are sometimes called Witherslack damsons after the village of that name (Mabey, 1978). Other names that have been recorded are Kendal Damsons, Westmoreland Prunes, and Lythe Valley Damsons. Recipes for damsons include jams and cheeses; the fruit is also used to flavour beer and gin.

TECHNIQUE:

Cumbria contains several sub-regions, including the Lake District; the Lythe Valley drains the south-eastern part of this. Climate is moderated by proximity to the sea to give high rainfall and relative warmth at sea-level. The valleys provide shelter for the trees, many of which are planted in alkaline soils, on steep marginal farmland, with south-eastern aspect.

Little systematic attention has been given in recent years to the orcharding of damsons in this area and many trees are now very old. The habit of planting them as hedgerow trees, or in orchards on hillsides, makes them difficult and time-consuming to harvest. As the orchards have become neglected, trees have weakened and blown down, leaving those still standing more exposed. For replanting, stock is usually obtained by taking suckers from old trees. Recently, with encouragement from the Countryside Commission, interest in damsons as a crop in the area has revived and some orchards have been replanted with appropriate varieties, both for the sake of the crop and for their value as a feature of the landscape, especially in spring when the trees are in blossom. The fruit are sold by the 'score' (20 lb, 9.1kg) in local markets and from the roadside during the season.

REGION OF PRODUCTION:

NORTH WEST ENGLAND, CUMBRIA.

Black Peas

DESCRIPTION:

SOLD DRIED, LOOSE FROM ANIMAL FEED VENDORS, OR IN PACKS FROM GROCERS AND SUPERMARKETS; OR OFFERED COOKED IN PORTIONS OF

ABOUT 75–100G. COLOUR: DEEP GREY-BLACK. FLAVOUR: EARTHY, COOKED-BEANS, USUALLY EATEN HEAVILY SEASONED WITH VINEGAR.

HISTORY:

Pulses, formerly a staple of the British diet, have lingered on, especially in Lancashire where black peas, *Pisum sativum*, are sold in the markets of the industrial towns to the north and east of Manchester. Oral tradition states that this has been the case for as long as anyone can remember; the dish is well-known locally, but is unknown in southern Britain.

A similar custom was recorded in the North East until the early years of the last century. It now appears extinct. The habit of consuming pigeon peas on Carling Sunday (the fifth in Lent) has been reported for many years, at least since the Tudor period (*OED*). Some link name and custom to Northumberland alone, but it was known throughout northern England. The peas were par-cooked in water and finished in lard.

Everywhere the peas are eaten, they are said to have first arrived as cargo on a ship driven ashore in a storm. Peter Brears (1987), in a discussion of Carling peas, remarks that this is probably apocryphal, as the peas are known far inland and the legend is recounted in several places. However, the pigeon peas used for this dish are a tropical crop, from Africa or the West Indies. There may be other, more tenuous links with seafaring, as brown beans seasoned with vinegar and syrup and served with fried salt pork are known as a Lenten dish in Sweden (ICA, 1971). The late Roy Shipperbottom, an expert on Lancashire food, remarks that black peas were served at fairs, and that Mrs Abbott's 'Black Pea Saloon (Quality, Cleanliness and Civility)' was a feature of Bolton New Year Fair.

Their consumption seems to be most persistent in areas where the pattern of urban working-class life led to a demand for ready-cooked food. Eunice Schofield (1975) mentions cooked peas as takeaway food in Jarrow, and black peas in Blackburn. According to Julia Smith (1989), Carling peas were placed on the bar in pubs in Driffield (East

Yorkshire) during the early part of Lent. They were prepared with extra salt to encourage thirst. As is perhaps apt for a foodstuff with so regional a pattern of affection, it goes under several names: parched peas (north Lancashire), pigeon peas, grey peas, and carlins or carlings (Northumberland, Durham, North Yorkshire).

TECHNIQUE:

Grey peas is a misnomer; what is actually required is the small brown pigeon pea. These can be found pre-packed in the markets and supermarkets of Lancashire as 'Black Peas', complete with a small tablet of bicarbonate of soda. They are bought, either to cook at home, or by vendors who sell them as a hot dish in the market halls. They are soaked for 24 hours in cold water with bicarbonate of soda added. The peas are boiled in the soaking water until they are deemed cooked. According to Samantha Saunders, a vendor of black peas, this judgement varies from area to area. In some towns, they are preferred whole, just soft when the skins have started to loosen, and are eaten cold. In others, they are cooked to a mush. Vendors keep the peas hot in the liquor or water in which they are cooked and sell them as portions in disposables, which have replaced the thick pottery cup once used. The customer adds vinegar. Carling peas were made by draining the cooked peas and finished by 'parching' them in large tins of lard seasoned with salt and pepper.

REGION OF PRODUCTION:

North West England.

Cheshire Cheese

DESCRIPTION:

Pressed cow's milk cheese. White Cheshire and red Cheshire are essentially the same cheese, except that annatto is added to the latter. Some is allowed to develop blue mould, in which case it is known as blue Cheshire. Blue Shropshire, a cheese created in the late 1970s, is of the same type. Cheshire

Cheese is produced in cylinders; the traditional size was about 22cm diameter by 26cm high, but weights now range from 500g to 25kg. Block Cheshire is also extensively produced. Colour: white Cheshire is a very pale cream colour; the 'red' is a pale pinky-orange; the blue is a pale creamy orange with heavy blue-grey veining. Flavour: both white and red are salty, crumbly and moist; the blue develops a sharper flavour, with a nutty aftertaste.

HISTORY:

Cheshire is one of a family of cheeses from west Cheshire and the bordering parts of Wales and Shropshire. One factor which contributed to its distinctiveness is that the area is located on salt-bearing rock strata. This is said to lend a special flavour to the milk of the cattle which graze there. The mild, damp climate is ideal for pasture, in turn promoting high milk yields.

Cheese-making in this area has a long history. Rance (1982) speculates that cheese was made in the North West prior to the Roman conquest, and that cow's milk was used from an early date. He also notes that it is mentioned in the Domesday Book (1087). There are many early references, from the late sixteenth and early seventeenth centuries, to cheese from this specific region (*OED*).

The basic craft method used for making Cheshire was established by the eighteenth century. A complex finishing process was followed, including repeated skewerings, pressings, turnings, and rebandaging in progressively finer grades of cloth, plus external salting. Finally, the cheeses were stored in a room designed to maintain a high ambient temperature with a carpeting of sedge, hay or straw. Production of Cheshire flourished. Some farmers used a cooperative system, contributing milk to a communal dairy, a custom which continued until the 1950s. Cheese fairs were held in several major towns. Construction of canals encouraged the export of Cheshire to other parts of the country, notably the Midlands and Yorkshire as well as the large cities closer to home, Liverpool and Manchester.

During the late 1800s, competition for farmhouse cheeses came from industrial producers. The supply of expanding markets with raw milk also diverted their attention away from cheese. Farmhouse production continued, but fell throughout the first half of the last century. During 1939–45 the Ministry of Food encouraged a harder, drier version of the cheese, and the number of farmhouse makers declined still further. However, the modern method for making cylindrical farmhouse Cheshire is essentially that used in the eighteenth century. Only the finishing has changed, many now dipping their cheeses in wax after bandaging. Block versions are also now available.

The phenomenon of blue veining in Cheshire was known locally as 'green fade'. It was discouraged in previous centuries, although Rance (1982) observes that the moist, loose-textured curd and the finishing process must both have promoted mould growth. However, green-fade cheeses were thrown away, or kept for medicinal use, to be applied externally to wounds and sores. In the late nineteenth and early twentieth centuries, green fades became more widely appreciated. Research was undertaken to investigate which cheeses blued the best. In the 1960s a recipe was developed with the explicit aim of producing blue Cheshire.

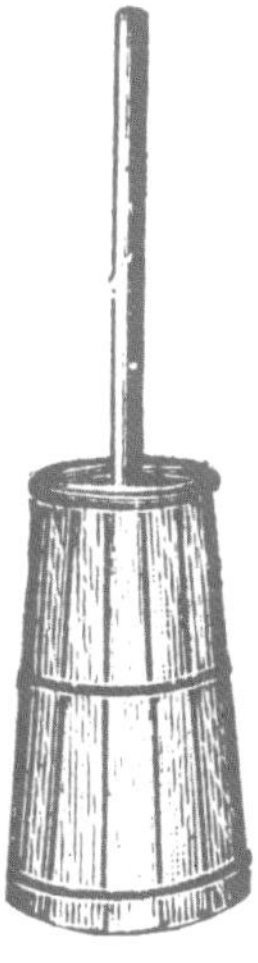

TECHNIQUE:

Craft method: details vary a little depending on the fat content of the milk, and whether a young or long-keeping cheese is desired. The milk is brought to 30°C. Specially cultured starter is added, typically 1.5–2 per cent, although up to 5 per cent may be added by some. If a red Cheshire is wanted, annatto is added. After 60–90 minutes rennet is added, and the surface stirred gently to prevent the fat rising. The curd is cut 3 ways to give particles the size of haricot beans. The temperature is raised gradually to 32°C, whilst the curd is stirred; this takes about 45 minutes. The curd is allowed to settle and the whey drained off. The curd is cut into blocks which are turned to the edge of the vat, leaving a central draining channel. When the acidity reaches the correct level, the blocks are broken in half and turned by hand; this process is repeated several times over a period of about 90 minutes. Salt is sprinkled over (about 1kg salt to 45kg curd). The curd becomes firm and dry and is milled when the acidity level is deemed correct; this depends on the final use of the cheese; an early-ripening cheese is milled at a higher acidity than one intended for long keeping. It is filled into moulds and pressed well down to consolidate, turned out again into coarse cloths, returned to the mould, and removed to a draining floor. The cheeses remain overnight, at 18°C, without any pressure being applied. Next day they are turned into clean smooth cloths. The cheeses are put under gradually increasing pressure for about 24 hours, then they are capped, bandaged and coated – traditionally with a flour paste, but now with either an edible cellulose paste or wax. They are ripened at 12°C, at a humidity of 85 per cent, turned every day. They are matured for 6–10 weeks.

Block farmhouse Cheshire is made from unpasteurized milk by the same method, but differences are imposed by the shape and the fact that the cheese will be matured and stored in plastic film. A drier curd is required, the cheese is pressed immediately after moulding, at a higher and more constant pressure than that used for farmhouse cheeses. Maturing is carried out at a lower temperature.

Blue Cheshire is now deliberately produced using a slightly more acid curd which is cut less finely and given a lighter pressure.

REGION OF PRODUCTION:

NORTH WEST ENGLAND.

Cumberland Rum Butter

DESCRIPTION:

A FLAVOURED BUTTER, SOLD IN QUANTITIES OF 110 OR 220G. COLOUR: A CREAM-YELLOW BROWN, DEPENDING ON THE TYPE OF SUGAR USED. FLAVOUR: SPICY, SWEET, ALCOHOLIC.

HISTORY:

Rum butter has been associated with Cumberland since at least the late nineteenth century, when Joseph Wright, collecting information for his *Dialect Dictionary*, noted the association of the dish with this region and several customs linked with it. Rum butter was 'eaten by wives during their confinement; and is offered to, and is expected to be partaken of, by visitors. The lady who first cuts into the bowl is predicted to require a similar compliment.' Coins for the baby were collected in the empty bowl. The *Oxford English Dictionary* gives the first instance of rum butter in print as Mrs A.B. Marshall's *Cookery Book* (1887). The recipe probably pre-dates this, as the ingredients are all traditional to Lake District cookery. It is also known in Cumbria as hard sauce. Today a brandy-flavoured version is also made.

TECHNIQUE:

Recipe and method are simple and vary only in the scale of operation from domestic kitchen to commercial confectioners. Unsalted butter is whipped to a cream, mixed with soft brown sugar and rum, and spiced to taste. The mixture is chilled until required. Light-brown or muscovado sugar can be used as taste dictates. The proportions are 1 part butter to 2 parts sugar.

REGION OF PRODUCTION:

NORTH WEST ENGLAND, CUMBRIA.

Lancashire Cheese

DESCRIPTION:

PRESSED COW'S MILK CHEESE, MADE IN 2 SIZES, EITHER WITH A DIAMETER OF ABOUT 30CM, WEIGHING ABOUT 23KG; OR A DIAMETER OF 16CM, ABOUT 12CM HIGH, WEIGHING APPROXIMATELY 5.5KG. THE TRADITIONAL SHAPE IS A TALL CYLINDER. COLOUR: A CLEAR PALE CREAMY YELLOW. FLAVOUR AND TEXTURE: CREAMY IN TEXTURE; THE FLAVOUR VARIES FROM MILD TO STRONG DEPENDING ON AGE.

HISTORY:

Lancashire cheese had become a distinct style, made in the centre of the county, by the eighteenth century. The traditional method is complex and time-consuming, requiring curd made on one day to be divided and mixed with that made the day before or the day after. This allows sufficient acidity to develop. According to *Law's Grocer's Manual* (*c.* 1895), portions of curd were sometimes kept for 4 or 5 days. Starter cultures were not introduced until the twentieth century, and were only used in very small proportions.

The first creamery Lancashire appeared early last century. Farmhouse cheese-making survived until 1939–45 but ceased because of regulations about use of milk for specific cheeses. It was revived on a limited scale in the late 1940s. By the early 1970s, a handful of farms were producing in the area traditionally associated with the craft. Lancashire is fragile. Almost all is produced around Preston, Chipping, and Garstang. It does not travel well and there is a strong preference for it on its home ground. The slowness and complexity of the method have inhibited creamery production. A block version was criticized by Patrick Rance (1982) who commented on the 'recent abuse' of the name: 'The real Lancashire was and remains a semi-soft, loose textured, crumbly, buttery cheese, unlike any other in flavour and resembling only the softer dales cheeses in consistency.' It retains a strong regional identity. It can be eaten alone but is excellent for cooking, especially toasting. 'Leigh Toaster' is an old name. In the past, a sage-flavoured Lancashire was made for Christmas. Beacon Fell Traditional Lancashire Cheese has been awarded PDO status.

TECHNIQUE:

Craft method: starter is used in very small proportions in the evening milk; then morning milk is mixed in and brought to 29°C. The vat is covered and the milk left to ripen for 45 minutes; rennet is added and stirred (to prevent the cream from separating) until coagulation. The vat is covered again and the curd left to firm for 45 minutes. It is cut into pieces the size of small beans and the whey drawn off. Then the curd is cut into blocks and scooped into a drainer in which it is pressed hard enough to release the whey but not so hard that the fat is lost. During this process the curd is broken by hand at intervals and the

Having long been a devoted fan of Kirkham's excellent Lancashire cheese, I was finally able to arrange a visit to the farm by combining it with an opportunity to see an Albert Irvin exhibition in Lancaster. It therefore didn't take too much persuasion before I was blasting out of London on my motorcycle early one clear but cold spring morning a few years ago. I pulled up in the farmyard at about 10.30 a.m. having ridden fairly briskly and was met by Graham, the cheesemaker and son of the much-heralded Mrs. Ruth Kirkham. As I removed my helmet, the conversation went something like this:

G: *(in very strong north Lancashire accent)* 'So where did you stop over last night?'

B: 'What do you mean?'

G: 'Where did you sleep last night?'

B: 'At home in London – I left this morning.'

G: 'But where did you *stop over*?'

B: 'I didn't; I came up this morning on the bike!'

G: *(calling excitedly and loudly into the farmhouse)* 'Mum, Mum come out here – Bruce is here' – she rushes out – '...look, I can't believe you're standing here in front of us now and you were in London this morning. How on earth did you get up here – did you fly? It normally takes us the best part of a day to get down to London in the wagon.'

There ensued a tour of the farm and the dairy, followed by bacon sandwiches in the farmhouse kitchen and afterwards huge mugs of tea in front of the coal fire in the parlour. Ruth and Graham are naturally warm and convivial folk who would not dream of receiving guests without offering generous helpings of proper Lancashire hospitality.

Truly wonderful people and truly a world-class cheese.

Bruce Poole

CHEF AND PROPRIETOR, CHEZ BRUCE, LONDON

pressure gradually increased over about 90 minutes. At this stage, the curd can either be stored in the vat to add to the next day's curd or added to that from the previous day; the batch is usually divided in half to preserve continuity. This process, known as the 'two-day curd' method, helps to give Lancashire cheese its unique identity. Occasionally, a three-day curd method is used on the same principles. The curd which is destined for cheese that day is salted (750g to 45kg curd) and milled twice. After the second milling, the curd is put into cloth-lined moulds and left to drain overnight. It is left under light pressure for 2 days, during which the cloths are changed twice, then the cheese is bandaged and returned to the press for another 12 hours. The cheeses are ripened at 13°C, turned daily. Then they are kept for varying lengths of time, according to the strength of flavour desired. These are mild (1–4 weeks), creamy (4–8), tasty (8–16), and strong (16 and over).

An industrial version is sold under the name of Lancashire. However, the step of keeping some curd back, essential to the flavour and texture of the cheese, is omitted. The result is sharp and crumbly and is called 'acid Lancashire'; it dominates the market in volume.

REGION OF PRODUCTION:

North West England, Lancashire.

Ribblesdale Cheese

DESCRIPTION:

Pressed, pasteurized-milk cheese. Cow's, goat's and sheep's versions are made – plain, smoked, or with garlic. Weight (approximate): sheep: 1.25kg; goat: 1.7kg; cow: 2kg. Form: flat wheels. Colour: almost white curd; waxed. Flavour: firm, nutty and mild.

HISTORY:

Ribblesdale, on the west of the Pennines, probably shared the general cheese-making tradition of the dales. The area has long been known for mild pressed cheeses. Both sheep and cow milk types are recorded.

No documentary evidence for cheese-making in the dale has been found, but artefacts such as a stone weight from a press at Ashes farm (where Ribblesdale cheese is now made) indicate that it was made there in the past. The modern cheese was evolved by the Hill family, using Wensleydale recipes, during the early 1980s.

TECHNIQUE:

The milk for the goat and cow cheeses comes from local suppliers; the sheep's is from further afield. It is curdled with starter, followed by vegetable rennet. The curd is always cut, but the particle size depends on the qualities of the milk from season to season; the curd is then scalded and salted before milling. The curd is filled into a mould and pressed for 48–72 hours. Maturation is 3–12 weeks; the cheeses are wax-dipped early in the maturing process.

REGION OF PRODUCTION:

North West England, Ribblesdale (Yorkshire).

Char (Windermere)

DESCRIPTION:

Char are a fish similar to trout, with reddish skin on the underside; they are noted for their delicate flavour.

HISTORY:

The char, *Salvinus alpinus*, is popularly associated in Britain with Windermere. The salt-water fish is known as the Arctic char, but land-locked populations survive in lakes throughout Europe (left behind as the waters receded after the Ice Age). Its range is limited to deep lakes whose waters maintain a temperature well below 20°C in summer. The *omble chevalier* of Lake Geneva is the most celebrated of these relics. There are few such lakes in England, all in the North West, but it is also found in some places in Wales, where it is known as *torgoch*, and Scotland. Mrs Beeton (1861) said the 'largest and the best kind is found in the lakes of Westmoreland, and, as it is considered a rarity, it is often potted and preserved.' There are many early references to char as a delicacy: it was sent in barrels to the royal court in the fifteenth century and mentioned in the form of pies in the seventeenth. The pie seems to have been the first method of preserving the food. Surviving correspondence from the Restoration period indicates that giant pies were sent down to London to give exiled Cumbrians a taste of home, or to persuade politicians of the worth of an applicant's cause. However, some time between 1670 and 1680, the experiment was made of substituting pottery for pastry, and the potted char was born. Not many years later, the intrepid traveller, Celia Fiennes, appreciated char potted with sweet spices by an innkeeper in Kendal in 1698 (Wondrausch, 1995).

It is to the custom of potting that the fish probably owe their fame. Potted fish was a storeroom constant before rapid transport and refrigeration permitted distribution to all classes in all places. To be stable in any climate, fish needed to be either salted, dried, smoked, pickled or potted. All these methods were pursued in early British kitchens, if for no other reason than to avoid monotony of flavour.

There was a whole industry for potting char. The fish were cleaned, spiced and packed in attractive dishes made especially for the purpose, then covered with butter and cooked. In this form they kept well and were exported to the rest of Britain. The fishery was in decline by 1860, due to overfishing by netsmen. Stocks recovered slightly as a result of official restrictions (ultimately all netting was forbidden), but they have never reached their former heights. Some fish are still taken. Char are now usually grilled for lunch or dinner. Potted char is made only at home or in restaurants and is rarely seen for sale.

TECHNIQUE:

On Windermere, a distinctive method of fishing is employed. It requires a rowing boat to support 2 rods, each of which bears a vertical line weighted with 750g lead weights. At intervals from each vertical line, 6 horizontal lines are trailed, each bearing 6–10 spinners or lures, the theory being that fish swimming at different depths can be caught. The boat has to be kept in constant motion so that the lines trail correctly and do not become tangled.

REGION OF PRODUCTION:

North West England, Windermere.

Potted Shrimps

DESCRIPTION:

Potted shrimps are composed of shelled, cooked shrimps covered with spiced butter. The shrimps have a salty, sweet, shellfish flavour; the butter is flavoured with spices to taste. Mace is customary. Benzoic acid, of neutral flavour, is sometimes added as a preservative.

HISTORY:

This has been a speciality of Morecambe Bay since at least 1799, the date of foundation of Baxter's, one of the producers of potted shrimps today. There is also a smaller trade in potted shrimps based on East Anglian ports.

TECHNIQUE:

Boiled shelled shrimps are added to spiced butter, allowed to cook briefly, chilled and packed into tubs which are then sealed with a little more butter.

REGION OF PRODUCTION:

North West England, Morecambe (Lancashire).

Shrimp (Morecambe Bay)

DESCRIPTION:

Maximum length 6cm. Colour: translucent reddish brown when alive, opaque pink-brown when cooked. Flavour: salty, with a mild, fishy sweetness and close texture.

HISTORY:

Shrimps, *Crangon crangon*, are abundant and easily caught in the shallow waters found on various parts of the British coast. Morecambe Bay is famous for them. David Stocker (1988) notes the existence of a subsistence fishery in the Morecambe Bay area since at least the late eighteenth century. This developed rapidly after the mid-nineteenth century, when a railway was built connecting the town to a wider market for sale of produce and reception of visitors. Shrimps were a fashionable food at this time, much in demand for afternoon tea. Michael Marshall (1987) observes that distinctive boats, known since the time of the First World War as 'nobbies', are associated with this fishery. There is also a substantial shrimp fishery in parts of the bay which relies on tractors (replacing the horses and carts used in earlier decades). Cedric Robinson is guide to the estuary sands; he is also one of a family which used horses to fish for shrimps. He remarks that the quality of catch has declined in recent years, which he attributes to over-fishing in the 1950s when tractors were first used.

Other important grounds for shrimps are the Solway Firth, the Wash (East Anglia) and the Thames. The shrimps are often known by the name of the town where they are landed, for instance Flookburgh, Parkgate.

At Leigh on Sea (Essex) and in the Thames estuary generally, the shrimp fishery was carried on in boats rather than off the beach. There, too, the ground was treacherous: 'I once worked aboard a shrimper which went on a mud bank and broke up. Every man knew there was only one thing left for him this side of death, and that was to sink slowly in the black ooze of the bank till it covered his head,' reported one old fisherman (Dyson, 1977). The fishermen of Leigh had a secret weapon in their exploitation of the shrimp. Early in Victoria's reign one of their number fitted a boiler in his boat so the catch was cooked on board without the need to set up a shore-based process. Marketing was the more direct and rapid. By 1850, there were 100 boats out of Leigh. The fishery declined thereafter (Dyson, 1977).

TECHNIQUE:

At low tide, well over 200 square kilometres of sand and mud are exposed in Morecambe Bay, deposited by 2 large rivers and several smaller streams which empty into the Irish Sea at this point.

Extremely dangerous for those without local knowledge, they include areas of quick-sand which change unpredictably, and the tide comes in fast, trapping the unwary. The village of Flookburgh is the centre of shrimp fishing from tractors; the fishermen set out as the tide ebbs, as soon as the water becomes shallow enough to ford the channels and creeks that cross the sands. For shrimping, long nets with a float at the cod end (the closed end which holds the catch) are hung from outriggers on a bogey or wheeled trailer. The whole arrangement is aligned so that the bogey and net are several metres beyond the water-line, even submerged under the water, attached by a long line to the tractor, which is driven slowly along the water-line. Periodically the net is emptied, the catch riddled or sieved and small and immature fish returned to the sea. On return to the shore, the shrimps (or prawns, also caught in this area) are boiled in sea water, riddled again, shelled if necessary, and packed.

REGION OF PRODUCTION:

North West England, Morecambe (Lancashire).

Herdwick Sheep

DESCRIPTION:

New-season Herdwick lamb has a dressed carcass weight of about 16kg; the wethers (castrated males over 1 year old) yield 20–21kg. The meat is dark, fine-grained, tender and very lean. Flavour is slightly gamy.

HISTORY:

Herdwick sheep are the traditional breed of the Lake District. They have distinctive white heads and legs; the lambs are born with black wool which greys with age. Their origins are unknown; a link with Scandinavian breeds has been suggested on genetic grounds. Their hardiness was noted in the late eighteenth century. The defining characteristics of the breed were established in the 1840s, but the Herdwick Breeders Association was only founded in 1916. Then,

Herdwicks were found over a wide area of Cumbria, but they are now reduced to the central and western parts of the Lake District. The breed was kept alive by the efforts of the writer Beatrix Potter. She bequeathed the farms and flocks she owned in the region to the National Trust, on condition this breed was kept on the land in perpetuity.

TECHNIQUE:

Herdwick sheep are exceptionally hardy. They spend their lives outdoors in the harsh climate of the hill tops, living on the native vegetation which includes lichens, heather and bilberries. It is to this diet that the good flavour is attributed. Little or no supplementary feed is given. The lambs are born in April and May, and reared outdoors by their mothers. The sheep are noted for their homing ability, and have a tendency to return to the patch of land on which they were reared. Although many Herdwicks are killed in the autumn of their first year to produce lamb, a proportion of wethers are over-wintered and slaughtered at 18–24 months to give meat with a stronger, more distinctive flavour. These older sheep are kept on the hill tops until late summer, and then brought to lower levels and finished on grass. The new season's lamb becomes available in September, and continues until about May; the wether mutton is available from late summer until May or June.

REGION OF PRODUCTION:

North West England, Lake District.

Black Pudding

DESCRIPTION:

Blood pudding, usually sausages 35–60mm diameter, 60–150 mm long, but sometimes baked in trays 60mm deep, or a slicing sausage about 70mm diameter and 400mm long. The smaller sausages weigh 115–200g. Form: opposite ends of the pudding are sometimes tied together with string to form small 'berries',

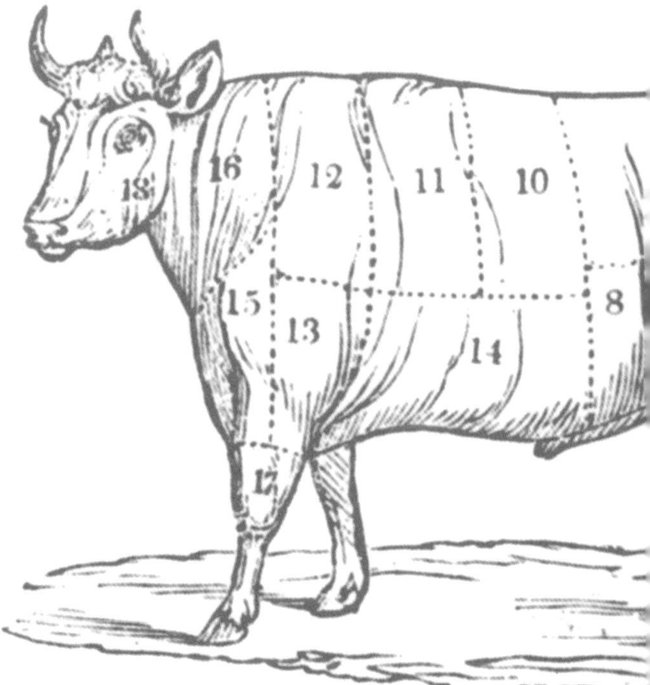

'Salads and eggs, and lighter fare,
Tune the Italian spark's guitar.
And, if I take Dan Congreve right,
Pudding and beef make Britons fight.'

MATTHEW PRIOR, *ALMA*

longer ones are shaped to form horseshoes or loops. Colour: the outside is black-brown, and may be rubbed with vegetable oil to give it a sheen; the cut pudding is a dark red-brown, studded with small pieces of white fat. Flavour: rich, savoury and spicy.

HISTORY:

The word pudding is of uncertain derivation and its relationship to the French word *boudin* unclear. It seems always to have carried a meaning of a mixture enclosed in a casing of animal gut. The English black pudding and the French *boudin noir* are obviously related but have developed along different lines.

Blood, especially pig's blood, was recorded in combination with cereals by both Homer and Apicius in classical times. It is safe to assume the inhabitants of the British Isles followed similar practices although no direct evidence has survived. Blood puddings are described in cookery books and manuscripts in Britain in the Middle Ages and an explicitly 'black' pudding crops up in the 1500s (*OED*).

They were made all over the country and were certainly consumed by people in all walks of life. The courtesan Harriette Wilson writes in her memoirs (1825) of 2 sisters visiting in Mayfair. 'Oh! by-the-bye, I forgot to order any dinner, and my maid and man are both out … However I can soon manage to get a black pudding broiled. You will not mind running to South Audley-street for a pound of black pudding? Shall you, my dear?'

As blood puddings were universal in Britain, it is not clear why the products of Lancashire should now be so pre-eminent. Stretford and Bury both developed reputations for the excellence of their puddings. There is plenty of evidence for them being made in Bury from at least the 1820s, and the presumption must be that manufacture long antedated that. The Thompson family, who still sell puddings in Bury market, trace their recipe back to 1865, and a shop called Casewell's, demolished in 1968, also claimed a very old recipe, never wittingly changed (Pollard, 1991). The concentration of large numbers of urban poor in the North West evidently increased the demand for cheap meat products and offal – see the entries for tripe (pp. 36-38). The many Irish immigrants, who had a tradition of such delicacies in their birthplace, must also have acted as stimulus. The difference between Lancashire puddings and those elsewhere revolved round variations in seasoning. *Law's Grocer's Manual* (*c.* 1895) listed seasonings for Cheshire, Shropshire, Staffordshire, Yorkshire and Stretford. Finney's manual for pork butchers (1915) listed the 'far-famed' Bury, Stretford, North Staffordshire, Cheshire and Yorkshire. Stretford and Bury mixtures each contained marjoram, thyme, pennyroyal and mint. Bury added celery seed. Staffordshire enjoyed the taste of pimento and coriander, as did Cheshire – with the extra zing of caraway. Yorkshire's cocktail consisted of thyme, marjoram, savoury and lemon thyme.

Regional distinctions have now lessened or been masked by brand names. Modern black puddings have also been affected by developments in pig breeds and by the requirements of public hygiene. Pigs are now bred to be lean and this has resulted in a diminution of the preferred leaf fat and increased the use of back fat. Considerations of hygiene have affected the use of fresh blood. Pig blood, which has good setting qualities, is now excluded because the pig has been found to urinate on slaughter, contaminating the blood. Tube-handled knives have been developed to overcome this problem, but butchers and health inspectors are suspicious of the technique. Fresh blood used in black puddings is now almost invariably ox blood. Dried blood is commonly used, and is approved by health officials.

Black puddings are eaten at breakfast, and widely served in hotels as part of an English fried breakfast. They are less commonly available at other meals except in the North. They are also popular street food in some places; the Black Pudding Stall sells hot puddings, eaten as people walk around Bury market, and they are also available at fairs and shows in Lancashire. When served as takeaways, they are split and served with mustard.

TECHNIQUE:

A typical black pudding mixture is 2.8kg groats or pearl barley, 2kg leaf or back fat, 1.5kg barley flour or fine oatmeal, 750g onions, 750g farina or rusk, 90 litres blood, 300g salt, 100g pepper. Seasonings vary according to the locality and are the only real distinguishing feature, beyond the care and skill of individual makers. In Bury, the seasoning for the mxture given above is 900g marjoram, 600g thyme, 450g pennyroyal and 500g bruised celery seed. Seasonings are added as ground or rubbed dried herbs. The barley is tied in a bag and boiled until cooked; whilst it is still hot the seasoning, flour and onion are added. The diced fat (which may be lightly sautéed) is mixed in, the blood added and the mixture thickened with oatmeal. The casings are filled, shaped and tied. Skins made from ox intestines are preferred, as the finished puddings fold into more elegant loops than those made from collagen or synthetic materials. The puddings are simmered in water at a temperature near boiling for 25 minutes; in some districts, a dye is added to give a more intense black. The puddings are then cooled and ready for sale. Although they are already cooked, puddings are always reheated at home by boiling gently, grilling, frying or baking.

REGION OF PRODUCTION:

North West England.

Cowheel

DESCRIPTION:

Cooked cowheels are inelegant, long rags of pale creamy-white skin and gristle, usually with the bones showing. Flavour: bland; it is the gelatinous texture which is valued.

HISTORY:

Calves' feet were delicacies – treated like pigs' trotters or made into a delectable jelly – or they were useful reinforcements to fine cookery, in stews or stocks or sauces. Cowheel was altogether more substantial: strongly gelatinous and containing much gristle, it took a long time to become tender. An early mention in a work by the seventeenth-century physician Thomas Moufet shows it was considered a valuable restorative, but generally it did not figure in dainty cookery books. Martha Bradley (1756) was one of the few who proposed using cowheel at genteel tables, 'though it may have an ordinary sound, [it makes] a very rich and fine soup, few exceeding it'. Apart from occasional appearances in standard Victorian works such as Mrs Beeton (1861), it was probably mostly left to the poor.

It is usually boned before eating; cowheel can be eaten cold with vinegar and salt; or cut up and made into a stew with a white sauce, or added to a richer mixture with beef and vegetables. The historian Robert Roberts (1971) was brought up in a corner shop in the working-class district of Salford (Lancashire). He recalled how 'relishes', or tasty little morsels that were for the father's tea alone, were part of their stock-in-trade: 'brawn, corned beef, boiled mutton ... saveloys, tripe, pig's trotters, sausage, cow heels ...' The French, by contrast, must sometimes have seemed to have used all their cowheels in *tripes à la mode de Caen*. However, the account in Charles Dickens' *The Old Curiosity Shop* of a supper cooked at the Jolly Sandboys inn may dispel the view that such dishes were French alone: '"It's a stew of tripe," said the landlord, smacking his lips, "and cowheel," smacking them again, "and bacon," smacking them once more, "and steak," smacking them for the fourth time, "and peas, cauliflowers, new potatoes, and sparrow-grass, all working together in one delicious gravy."'

By the 1940s and 1950s, cowheel was associated with the North Country, where Hartley (1954) remarked it was a favourite stand-by in cattle-market towns, and was made into a jellied brawn. Cowheels were prepared by tripe dressers; Roger Taulbman, president of the National Association of Tripe Dressers says this is because, in the past, a 'tripe set' of offals from a cow consisted of the tripe, feet, reed and weazand or windpipe. Already, in 1762, the advice was, 'take a cowheel from the Tripe House ready drest.' (*OED*)

TECHNIQUE:

Cowheels come from animals over about 8 months old (any younger, and they are classed as calves and have smaller, more delicate feet). After washing, scalding and removal of the hair and hooves, they are cooked by boiling for 3–4 hours, then cooled, drained and bleached.

REGION OF PRODUCTION:

North West England, Lancashire.

Cumberland Ham

DESCRIPTION:

An unsmoked, cured ham for cooking. The skin is a pale cream-gold, the lean a deep, translucent red when raw and mid-red to pale pink when cooked, the fat is white. Those produced today weigh in the region of 7.5kg. Flavour and texture: a deep, pronounced ham flavour, slightly spicy, heavily salted, with a close, relatively dry texture.

HISTORY:

Lake District ham has had a good reputation for 200 years. The county of Westmoreland appears to have been noted for it when Nicholson and Burn (1777) wrote of it being cured in the smoke of a peat fire. Mrs Beeton (1861) gave a recipe, 'to cure sweet hams in the Westmoreland way', using a mixture of salt, sugar, bay salt and beer; the ham was to be pickled 1 month and smoked 1 month. Fifty years later, in *Law's Grocer's Manual*, it was Cumberland, not Westmoreland, which was recognized as the regional name associated with hams. Douglas's *Encyclopaedia* also observed that Cumberland was an area noted for ham curing. These hams owed some of their special character to the local pigs. An unimproved breed, they were kept by farmers and cottagers and allowed to scavenge the farmyard and woodland. Their diet was supplemented with household waste, often with plenty of potato peelings. Towards the end of their lives, they were fed on oats and became extremely fat. Killed in winter, the meat was divided up and parts of it, including the hams, reserved for curing at home. The modern Cumberland ham is not well known outside its native region.

TECHNIQUE:

After being separated from the carcass, the hams are dry-salted for 1 month with salt and salt-petre; they are then dried and matured at ambient temperature for 3 months before sale. They are no longer smoked.

REGION OF PRODUCTION:

North West England, the Lake District.

Cumberland Sausage

DESCRIPTION:

A long, unlinked, uncooked fresh pork sausage of lean and fat pork (typically 85–95 per cent of the filling), 2–3cm diameter, 2–3 metres long. Colour: when uncooked, a pale grey-pink. Flavour: rich pork taste, generally highly spiced with black pepper, spices and herbs.

HISTORY:

Cumberland sausage, whilst belonging to the tradition of British fresh meat sausages, is recognized as a distinct type. Its history is largely undocumented. English fresh sausages are usually divided into links about 12cm long, a habit which has been followed ever since the early seventeenth century (Wilson, 1973). For some reason, this tradition was not pursued in the North West and the sausage was measured and sold by the yard. Until the turn of the twentieth century, Richard Woodall's shop in Waberthwaite had had two drawing pins on the counter for measuring the sausage. All that can be said from information available at present is that this sausage has been made in the region for the last 100 years and is thought typical of the area. Correspondence in *Cumbria Magazine* (1957) mentions Cumberland sausages 'about 30 years ago' and remarks that they were 'bigger and better ... with a flavour entirely different to any others'. James Cranston, whose family set up a butcher's business in the area before the First World War, remarks that sausages are invariably made with a high meat content.

TECHNIQUE:

A Cumberland breed of pig did exist but is now extinct. Small butchers in the area use locally reared commercial breeds. The meat is coarsely chopped, originally by hand but now mechanically. The method is similar to other British fresh sausages: a simple mixture of raw chopped pork, seasoning and rusk is used to fill sausage skins, but the meat content is typically very high, up to 98 per cent of the filling and, once filled, the sausage is left as a long piece, not twisted into links. Black and white pepper, marjoram, nutmeg and mace are perhaps the major seasonings (Poulson, 1979); sage is used by many butchers.

REGION OF PRODUCTION:

North West England, Cumbria.

Cumbria Air Dried Ham

DESCRIPTION:

An unsmoked cured ham for eating raw. The skin is pale cream-gold, the lean deep, translucent red. Weight: about 6kg. Flavour: intense salt ham with slight sweetness.

HISTORY:

Hams made in Britain are usually cooked before eating. However, the continental raw hams have long been well known and highly regarded and there has always been a market for them. During the twentieth century, legal status aimed at preventing the spread of notifiable diseases amongst farm animals meant that imports of raw ham from abroad were limited, so the development of home-produced types was a logical step.

Cumbria air-dried ham is an emergent regional food. In this particular case, Woodall's, the company which created the ham, has a history stretching back to the early 1800s when they began as bacon-curers. Cumbria air-dried ham is firmly rooted in a long tradition of taking foreign ideas and techniques and turning them into a distinctively British affair.

Cumbria Mature Royal Ham, made by the same company, is another emergent product, based on a mid-nineteenth century recipe from Suffolk. This was brought to Cumberland in the 1920s by the mother of the present chairman. It is based on a brine cure containing molasses, which fits in well with the food traditions of the Lake District where the use of unrefined sugar is typical. It is also smoked, recalling the Westmoreland hams of the 1700s.

TECHNIQUE:

A dry cure is used. Carcasses from selected pigs are hung for at least a week, then butchered. The hams are laid on a slab for about a month with salt and saltpetre, then dried and hung to mature for 12 months.

REGION OF PRODUCTION:

North West England, Cumbria.

Herdwick Macon Ham

DESCRIPTION:

Whole, smoked, cured hams made from sheep meat weighing around 3kg (bone in) or 1.8kg (boned). Colour: very dark red, translucent lean with streaks of pale, creamy gold fat; dark gold outside. Flavour: pronounced gamy lamb flavour with herb undertones and mild smoke.

HISTORY:

The word ham is used in connection with cured pig meat in modern Britain, but it has a broader meaning of the hind leg of any animal, especially those killed for meat. Goat hams were cured in Wales and other regions until the late eighteenth century (Wilson, 1973) and badger hams were not unknown. The use of mutton (meat from a sheep over one year old) to make hams is also a long British tradition, which lingered in the more remote uplands.

The word macon was a hybrid (m[utton + b]acon) of the Second World War to describe mutton cured as bacon – an innovation that took advantage of an excess of highland sheep at a time when pigs were an increasing rarity. Another solution, adopted with enthusiasm by both the Ministry of Food and the population as a whole, was urban backyard pig-keeping, a skill that had fallen into desuetude since the industrial revolution.

Hannah Glasse (1747) gives instructions for dry-curing mutton hams with salt and sugar, followed by smoking and boiling. Recipes were also to be found in nineteenth-century books on curing meat (David, 1970). In the modern era, mutton hams were a rarity although the idea was preserved in some parts, notably the Lake District. Poulson (1978) collected an old recipe for brining a mutton ham in a mixture which included molasses and spices, before drying and smoking. Until recent years, they were produced by only a few families for their own use. Modern interest in unusual foods has led to a revival of commercial production by a company based at Corney (Cumbria). The preserved ham would once have been soaked and boiled, then eaten with bread at ordinary meals. Those made today are eaten raw – the manufacturer suggests with fruit in the manner of Italian air-dried hams.

TECHNIQUE

A local sheep breed, the Herdwick, provides the meat. They are killed at 2–3 years. Cross-bred sheep are used to provide larger hams. The hams remain in a dry cure of spiced salt for about 3 weeks. They are cold-smoked over oak and juniper, then matured for 8 months.

REGION OF PRODUCTION:

NORTH WEST ENGLAND, CUMBRIA.

Pressed Beef

DESCRIPTION:

PIECES OF COOKED BEEF SET IN DARK BROWN JELLY, THINLY SLICED (ABOUT 5MM THICK) AND SOLD BY WEIGHT.

HISTORY:

This foodstuff is similar in concept to brawn. Like brawn, it probably began as something larger, more elaborate and more esteemed. The origins may lie in collaring, a way of preserving large, boned joints by brining and spicing, then rolling tightly in a cloth (collar) tied with tape or string, before boiling slowly. The meat could be preserved still longer if it were then potted under a layer of melted suet (Hartley, 1954). Early recipes for fine dishes of well-seasoned beef joints in jelly may also have influenced the development of this dish (David, 1970).

By the mid-nineteenth century, collaring was no longer fashionable, but jellied meats pressed into moulds and served cold (much as pressed tongue, another English favourite) had entered the repertoire of the cooked-meat counter as a way of using some of the less saleable cuts. *Dalton's Meat Recipes*, published in the 1930s, describes several products of the pressed-beef type, of varying degrees of sophistication. Mabey (1978) found the quantity and variety of cooked meats available in the industrial towns of Lancashire remarkable, mentioning amongst other items, 'various types of pressed meat in slices or moulds: beef, pork, lamb, chicken ... They are put into sandwiches, wedged into rolls, baps and barmcakes, or set out on plates for high tea.'

TECHNIQUE:

Pressed beef may use cheaper cuts from the forequarter, especially the brisket, which have excellent flavour but are not prime roasting material. The meat is covered with water and seasoned; old recipes call for the addition of cowheels. The whole is cooked gently for up to 3 hours, any bones removed and the meat put into a pudding basin. At this stage, if no cowheel was used, some butchers add gelatine to the stock poured over the meat. It is cooled, then pressed and the stock sets to a jelly.

REGION OF PRODUCTION:

North West England, Todmorden (Lancashire).

Tripe

DESCRIPTION:

Tripe is sold by weight. In appearance, on the slab, it is sheets of pale, cream-coloured tissue, in roughly-cut pieces 15–20cm square. The most distinctive type is honeycomb, which has a pattern of raised lines crossing the surface

HISTORY:

Internal organs were no doubt more important foods when meat was a luxury and all parts of a slaughtered animal were carefully utilized. The name tripe derives from Norman French, but some of the dialect words associated with it are of Teutonic origin. This would suggest that, even in the early Middle Ages, it was not thought of as utterly dainty or high-status (on the analogy of Norman French being the root language of aristocratic culinary usage, while Anglo-Saxon implies something more popular). It is mentioned in numerous texts from the fifteenth century onwards, and appears in Shakespeare's *Taming of the Shrew* in the line, 'How say you to a fat tripe finely broiled?'

There were plenty of ways to deal with it: boiled, with onion; broiled, with saffron fricassees; or dipped in batter and fried (Glasse, 1747; Bradley, 1756; Raffald, 1769). Samuel Pepys enjoyed it in the company of his wife in 1662, 'a most excellent dish of tripes of my own directing, covered with mustard, as I have here-to-fore seen them done at my Lord Crews.' It was held in some esteem, considered easily digested and thought to be good for invalids. As late as the 1950s, the British Medical Association publicized it as a nourishing dish.

Nourishing perhaps, but it was not often encountered on the tables of gentlefolk. Its presence usually indicates some form of dearth – it cropped up a lot during wartime rationing. In recent years it has suffered a drop in popularity along with most other sorts of offal and is now a minority taste.

Tripe's recent history, however, is most eloquent in the northern districts of Lancashire and Yorkshire. Here, the immense increase in an urban proletariat that needed cheap and easy feeding meant the survival of a number of otherwise unmentionable parts of cows, pigs and sheep. Tripe was one of the most popular. There were 260 specialist tripe shops in Manchester in 1906 and 76 shops in Bolton in 1911 (Shipperbottom, 1995). Like the fish fryers, they produced cheap, nourishing food.

Faced with a great increase in purveyors, the industrial towns speedily enforced the 1875 Public Health Act which designated tripe-boiling amongst the offensive trades and regulated the cleaning of premises in which it was carried on. This was stimulus to a concentration of businesses. In Lancashire, during the early 1900s, there were amalgamations of tripe dressers and agreements to improve and enhance the trade. Every Lancashire town had tripe shops, and some of these had restaurants. The Tripe de Luxe Restaurant in Wigan had a female musical trio, and seating for 300 in an oak-panelled room with chandeliers. Marjory Houlihan, in her pamphlet on the Lancashire tripe trade, notes that such establishments were flourishing as late as the 1960s, and describes a magnificent banqueting suite in one of them.

Tripe-boiling is now less important, partly due to the decline in the Lancashire cotton trade and the way of life associated with it; and partly because of competition from other foods. The large company, United Cattle Products, found their premises had a higher property value than the tripe business could justify and sold their sites. The declining number of outlets has had its effect on the trade, and there are far fewer tripe dressers. The requirements of public health regulations, which insist on expensive improvements to premises, has caused some to close and forced the price of tripe to rise.

Tripe is the English term for the stomach bags of animals,

especially cattle. The various parts of the tripe are given names which are often very localized. Some examples are: for the first stomach (*rumen*), thick seam, blanket; for the second (*reticulum*), honeycomb tripe; for the third (*omasum*), bible tripe, monkshood, psalterium, book, manifold, many-plies; for the fourth (*abomasum*), black or raggy tripe. The oesophagus is also treated as part of the tripe, and is known as weasand or bellrope. Pig's stomach is also eaten, but has only one chamber, similar to *abomasum* tripe.

Tripe in the north of England is cooked and ready to eat at point of sale. That sold in the South requires further cooking. Bleached tripe is the norm. Unbleached tripe is sometimes sold, but is now almost impossible to obtain. Tripe is consumed cold with vinegar and salt. Tripe and salad is a popular meal in hot weather, or it can be heated up in milk flavoured with onions, or made into more elaborate dishes to individual taste.

TECHNIQUE:

Preliminary cleaning is done at the abattoir, where the tripes are washed. They are then taken to specialist tripe dressers. The tripes are tumbled in a hot lime and soda solution which cleans, bleaches, and removes some of the fat and membranes. Removal of the outer skin (a process which was originally by hand with a scrubbing brush) is now done in a machine called a 'Parmentière', fitted with an abrasive drum. Boiling takes 2 hours or longer. Some areas only parboil the tripe. The tripes are steeped in a mild peroxide solution to whiten them further; then they are thoroughly washed. In the final dressing, the tripe is trimmed and made ready for sale.

REGION OF PRODUCTION:

NORTH WEST ENGLAND, LANCASHIRE.

Borrowdale Tea Bread

DESCRIPTION:

Baked in a loaf shape, a small deep oblong. Colour: dark brown, with paler crumb and dried fruit. Flavour and texture: sweet and aromatic, with a fairly dense, chewy texture.

HISTORY:

There are 2 reasons why this might be called tea bread: one is because the dried fruit used for making it is soaked in tea prior to mixing; the other is that it is suitable for eating with tea. Both are equally plausible. The reason for the persistent association of this type of fruited bread with the North-West is unknown. The most likely is the existence of commercial tourism from an early date. Tea-time specialities have been developed in most areas of Britain with a substantial tourist industry. In the Lake District tourism has been important since the early 1800s. Bakeries in the area also produce very plain fruit loaves using bread dough and dried fruit, without the preliminary step of soaking the fruit in tea. Domestic cooks of Borrowdale and district frown on this, saying the result is not as well flavoured and does not keep as well. However, plain breads may represent earlier types of this product, as tea cannot have been used as an ingredient for more than 200 years at the most, and this type of spiced and fruit dough has a much longer history.

TECHNIQUE:

Modern recipes for the loaf show it to be rather plain; it is leavened with baking powder. Flour, brown sugar, currants and raisins in the proportions 2:1:1:1 are used. The fruit, plus some candied peel and sugar are soaked overnight in cold tea. It is baked at 180°C for 60–90 minutes. Commercial bakers tend to produce a yeast-leavened version.

REGION OF PRODUCTION:

North West England, the Lake District.

Chorley Cake

DESCRIPTION:

Dimensions: approximately 80mm diameter, just over 10mm deep. Weight: about 75g. Colour: pale brown pastry, darker towards the edges, dark currant filling. Flavour: predominantly sweet currants, with crisp pastry.

HISTORY:

Chorley cakes are regarded by some as a poor relation of Eccles cakes. There are distinct similarities; both involve a filling of currants in a pastry crust. It is probable that they spring from a common tradition, although Eccles cakes are the more famous and better documented. The earliest known reference to Chorley cakes dates from the 1920s when a local newspaper editor reminisced about the 1880s. He recalled 2 sisters, the Misses Corbitt, who made Chorley cakes and sold them for 2d (1p) each, a high price at a time when a working man could expect to be paid about 15p a day. A trade directory in the town records a Miss Corbitt keeping a confectionery shop from at least 1874. The tradition of Chorley cakes has continued to the present day. Similar confections are made in nearby towns, using pastry left over from pie-making. One firm, Hall's, still makes the cakes in the town itself.

TECHNIQUE:

The cakes are made using short-crust pastry rolled to 50mm thick, and cut into rounds about 200mm across. A layer of currants is placed in the centre of each, the edges of the pastry brought together, and sealed. These are rolled lightly until the currants show through the pastry and the shape is a flattened round. They are baked at 180°C for 30 minutes.

REGION OF PRODUCTION:

North West England, Chorley (Lancashire).

Cumberland Rum Nicky

DESCRIPTION:

A circular tart, now also baked in long oblongs, with a decorative pastry lattice on top. Colour: a golden crust with dark, rich brown filling. Flavour: rich, soft filling with spices and rum.

HISTORY:

Rum Nicky contains elements present in British cookery for many centuries. Rum, the vital ingredient, has been imported from the West Indies into ports on the Cumbrian coast for at least 200 years. The filling contains dates and preserved ginger. It bears some resemblance to the combination of spice and dried fruit known as mincemeat, but also to mixtures proposed in sixteenth-century cookery books, such as one from 1587, of prunes with breadcrumbs, claret, ginger, and sugar.

Earlier last century, it was the form of the dish rather than the filling which distinguished it. In the 1930s, Mrs Arthur Webb recorded visiting a Lake District farmhouse on a day when nickies were being baked. She recorded that they were of several sorts (including some sounding very like mince pies or Eccles cakes), some were made with dough and some with shortcrust. The local method was to leave the edge plain, but make cuts or nicks to and fro across the top. As the present-day tart always involves a decoration of pastry trellis, it would seem that this, rather than the rum filling, is what gave the dish its identity. Several small bakeries continue to manufacture it; one at least has a large mail-order business at Christmastide.

TECHNIQUE:

Examples collected recently used either short-crust or puff pastry rolled to fill a shallow dish. The filling is chopped dates, preserved ginger, butter, sugar and rum. It is baked at 220°C for 10–15 minutes, followed by 30 minutes at 180°C.

REGION OF PRODUCTION:

North West England, Cumbria.

Eccles Cake

DESCRIPTION:

A FRUIT-FILLED PASTRY, 60–80MM DIAMETER, 20MM DEEP. WEIGHT: 30–40G. COLOUR: LIGHT BROWN PUFF OR FLAKY PASTRY OFTEN WITH GLIMPSES OF DARK CURRANTS; IN SOME VARIATIONS THE CURRANTS ARE CLEARLY VISIBLE THROUGH SLASHED CUTS ON THE TOP; THE SURFACE IS OFTEN GLAZED AND SPRINKLED WITH SUGAR. FLAVOUR: SWEET, WITH CRISP PASTRY AND RICH CURRANTS; A TYPICAL CAKE IS ABOUT 40 PER CENT CURRANTS TO 60 PERCENT PASTRY.

HISTORY:

Similar affairs of puff pastry with currant fillings exist in other parts of England but they are of different shapes and their historical relationship to the Eccles cake is unclear.

There is a myth that this particular recipe was given to a girl as she left the employ of Mrs Raffald, whose *English Housekeeper* was an important Georgian kitchen vade-mecum and who was a noted confectioner in Manchester nearby. It is certainly true that Raffald's book contains plenty of patties – some of which have currants in the filling – and that by a stretch of imagination an Eccles cake could be termed a patty (in fact those were much smaller), but the connection is exiguous. It is perhaps more germane to note that cakes were recorded before this time (the 1770s) as being sold at Eccles but that nobody wrote down their composition. They were a feature of the town wakes, a religious festival commemorating the foundation of the local church. Wakes Week used to be in September, but is now in July.

There has long been dispute about which family in the area produced the originals but the arguments settle no facts about antecedents or early history. By the early 1800s, however, there is evidence of an established pattern of wholesaling well beyond the town boundaries. By then, there were several makers and some were producing large numbers for sale. Surviving details from auctioneers' records mention that Birch's shop was making 5,000 cakes every day; and evidently the principal shop, Bradburns, baked 8,000. The cakes were popular at public events, especially sports meetings and at racecourses. There are also claims of a large export trade to America during this period.

A recipe from the first half of the nineteenth century calls for a spicy currant filling in a puff pastry case although other early recipes called for the currants to be mixed through the dough. *Law's Grocer's Manual* (*c*.1895) noted 'the great guiding principle' in Eccles cakes is currants, sweetness and lightness. It went on to say that cakes made in south Lancashire were often baked in a very hot oven, caramelizing the sugar on the outside. Recipes from professional manuals of the same date seem to treat Eccles and Banbury cakes as nearly identical, the main difference being shape: an Eccles cake is always round. No-one can deny a basic similarity, but comparison reveals very different products.

TECHNIQUE:

The essential characteristic of pastry for Eccles cakes is that it does not have as much 'lift' as other puff pastry products. Care is taken to avoid waxy, palate-clinging pastry. The better cakes are made with butter and only a small amount of scrap pastry (offcuts from earlier batches) is incorporated. The filling always includes currants (the best local maker uses Vostizza) and brown sugar; some add cake crumbs, chopped peel, spice and Golden Syrup. The pastry is cut into 100–120mm discs. The filling is placed centrally and the edges folded in to cover it. The pastry is turned over, slightly flattened, brushed with egg white or milk, sprinkled with sugar and 2 or 3 parallel cuts made on top. After resting for 40 minutes, it is baked at 225°C for 20–25 minutes.

REGION OF PRODUCTION:

North West England, Eccles (Lancashire).

Goosnargh Cake

DESCRIPTION:

A circular biscuit, 80mm diameter, 10mm deep. Weight: 50g. Colour: off-white, darker towards the edge, with dark

SPECKLES AND A THICK COATING OF FINE SUGAR. FLAVOUR AND TEXTURE: BUTTERY, CARAWAY SEEDS; A FINE, SHORT TEXTURE.

HISTORY:

Goosnargh is a village north of Preston. Butter, the essential ingredient of Goosnargh cakes, is a product of the region. The origin of the cakes is unknown. Their texture is close to shortbread, the ancestors of which were popular all over Britain in the sixteenth and seventeenth centuries. Caraway, in the form of whole seeds, was a common ingredient in contemporary biscuit and cake recipes. Beyond these general observations, these cakes cannot be traced other than from local historian Richard Cookson's observation in 1888 that 'Goosenargh has almost world-wide fame for making of penny cakes of a peculiar pastry, and great as the depression of trade at present is, about 4,000 dozens are disposed of annually about Whitsuntide.' This implies the cakes had been well known for years. The connection with the religious festival also speaks of a long usage: the area was conservative, preserving remnants of traditions associated with Catholicism long after they had vanished in other parts. Similar cakes were known in other towns in the region, baked at other times, often as fairings.

As with so many other British specialities requiring dairy produce, the cakes suffered from wartime rationing. Spicer (1948) remarked that Goosnargh (the name was often used without further qualification) had been almost impossible to make since the war, because of the large quantities of butter required. In recent years they have been made again and the old preference for caraway spicing – often jettisoned by modern bakers – has been continued. However, the link with Whitsuntide has vanished.

TECHNIQUE:

The ingredients are flour, butter, sugar, in the proportions 6:4:1. Flavourings are ground coriander and whole caraway seeds. The butter, sugar and spices are creamed, the flour is rubbed in and the mixture pressed into a coherent dough without any liquid. This is rolled out and cut into rounds with a plain cutter. The surface is sprinkled thickly with caster sugar. The raw biscuits are left to stand for at least 2 hours. They are baked at 140°C for 30–40 minutes. The cakes should be firm, but remain very pale. In airtight tins, they keep for several months.

REGION OF PRODUCTION:

North West England, Preston (Lancashire).

Grasmere Gingerbread

DESCRIPTION:

Oblong or square pieces of gingerbread; Sarah Nelson's Grasmere Gingerbread is thinner than other English gingerbreads and is made in pieces 80mm by 50mm, 8mm deep; other types are cut in squares or bars of varying size, about 15mm thick. Weight: Sarah Nelson's is cut in pieces of about 35g; other types are sold in pieces of around 50g. Colour: rich mid-brown; Sarah Nelson's has a sandy appearance. Flavour and texture: sweet, spicy, with hard, chewy texture; Sarah Nelson's has exceptional flavour of strong ginger with a bitter fruit note.

HISTORY:

Grasmere is a small town in the centre of the English Lake District. The nearby coast has several important harbours and formerly traded with the West Indian colonies and the port of Liverpool. Local cookery has an emphasis on rum, unrefined sugar and spices, especially ginger, which may derive from this trade. The grain used in the area until the nineteenth century was oats. Some types of gingerbread made in the north of England, including ones quoted in domestic cookery books under the title Grasmere, still call for it.

However, the earliest form of gingerbread in Grasmere may have been quite different. Brears (1991) refers to an entry in the church-wardens' accounts for 1819, recording payment for 'rushbearers' gingerbread'. This refers to the custom of carrying rushes to St Oswald's church, originally as floor covering but more recently as decoration. A succession of bakers in the town are recorded as providing gingerbread to the church as payment to the rushbearers. This confection, still made for the rushbearing on the feast of St Oswald (6 August), is not the type now associated with the town. The vicar says that it is thick and soft and is stamped with a rushbearing motif.

Dorothy Wordsworth writes in her Grasmere journal for 1803 (Clark 1960): 'W[illia]m had a fancy for some ginger bread … and we walked towards Matthew Newton's. I went into the house. The blind man and his wife and sister were sitting by the fire, all dressed very clean in their Sunday clothes, the sister reading. They took their little stock of gingerbread out of the cupboard, and I bought 6 pennyworth. They were so grateful when I paid them for it that I could not find it in my heart to tell them we were going to make gingerbread ourselves. I had asked them if they had no thick – "No," answered Matthew, "there was none on Friday, but we'll endeavour to get some." The next day the woman came just when we were baking and we bought 2 pennyworth.' This account seems to confirm both sorts of gingerbread, thin and thick, that are available today.

Grasmere gingerbread developed its current identity with the development of the tourist trade. In the 1850s, Sarah Nelson, a Lancashire woman, began to bake a Lancashire type of gingerbread for sale to locals and visitors. The present business which bears her name was established in 1854 in a small building formerly the village school. Her recipe has been the sole property of 3 families during the intervening years. Other recipes have been published in various cookery texts: they are generally for a type of shortbread, flavoured with ginger, and may or may not involve a portion of oatmeal. 'Sarah Nelson's Grasmere Gingerbread', the most famous variety, is a trademark. Others are sold simply as Grasmere gingerbread and, while they may share a common origin, are not exactly the same.

TECHNIQUE:

The method of making Sarah Nelson's Gingerbread is a trade secret and it is company policy to withhold information. Other recipes are for a simple shortbread mixture, using flour, butter and moist brown sugar in proportions of 8:5:4, ginger and baking powder. Some call for oatmeal in place of flour, and rub the butter into the mixture rather than melt it. This type of recipe and method is used by local bakers.

REGION OF PRODUCTION:

North West England, Grasmere (Cumbria).

Hawkshead Wig

DESCRIPTION:

An oval bread roll 70mm long, 40mm wide, 40mm deep. Weight: about 40g. Colour: golden with a shiny top. Flavour: a plain bread, lightly spiced with caraway.

HISTORY:

Wigs (sometimes spelled whigs or wiggs) were light-textured, white bread, raised with yeast. The origin of the name is not clear. It is possibly derived from a Teutonic word meaning wedge. In some later recipes the wigs are formed into rounds quartered by a cross, allowing them to be broken into wedges after baking. Both buns and wigs are fine white breads connected with Lent. Samuel Pepys wrote that he had a Lenten supper of wigs and ale in 1664. Buns were early defined as Lenten bread. The word possibly derives from the Old French *bugne*, later *beignet* – a small something which puffs up, as fine white bread leavened with yeast would do. Wigs were thought of in the same terms. They were obviously made with fine white flour, and a fifteenth-century reference equates them with buns. The Restoration herald Randle Holme defined wigs as white bread moulded longways and thick in the middle.

By the time we have recipes, they were sweetened, enriched with butter and usually spiced – with coriander (Nott, 1726) or caraway (the most common). *The Magazine of Domestic Economy* (1840) requires cream, butter, sugar and spices, including caraway seeds. Irrespective of the connection with Lent, wigs do crop up as a festive food eaten at particular times. Spicer (1948) recorded several special days at which wigs were eaten at different locations, including Christmas (Shrewsbury), St Catherine's (Buckinghamshire, where the wigs were an oblong shape) and St Andrew's (Bedfordshire).

From the 1850s they seem to be mentioned much less frequently. It is possible that the name simply went out of current use. A Victorian comment was that there were so many 'common buns' around that the word wig had been forgotten (David, 1977). Minwel Tibbott (1976) observes that in North Wales, the word wig was applied to the long narrow iced currant bun, made from a lightly sweetened dough known in the rest of the country as iced bun.

Florence White (1932) found that rolls known as wigs were still made and sold in the small town of Hawkshead. According to Phyllis Graham, a native, they are still known and occasionally made in the locality although little interest is taken in them. Only one commercial producer has so far been located.

TECHNIQUE:

Hawkshead wigs are plain and include lard – none of the sugar, butter and milk of many early recipes. An ordinary dough is set to rise; it is knocked back and softened lard (8 parts dough to 1 part lard) is kneaded in, together with a small quantity of caraway seeds. The mixture is scaled off into portions of about 40g, shaped into ovals, and allowed to rise again; the tops are brushed with milk and sugar. The buns are baked for 20–30 minutes at about 220°C.

REGION OF PRODUCTION:

North West England, Hawkshead (Cumbria).

Kendal Pepper Cake

DESCRIPTION:

Circular cakes, 30–40mm deep. Colour: dark, rich brown surface, speckled with currants, sugar and candied peel; interior paler, with a dry crumb; Flavour: sweet, bitter note from peel dominating, distinct spicy-pepper flavour.

HISTORY:

Pepper cakes belong to the general tradition of spiced, fruited cakes. This was originally a Christmas recipe and the connection of extravagant spices with festivities is hallowed. The use of pepper in this context is curious. There are 2 possible explanations. According to Wright (1896–1905), pepper originally meant a spicing of ginger in Northern counties. A similar usage is found in Sweden, where ginger biscuits are called *pepparkaker*. Alternatively, the name may have come from the use of allspice (*Pimenta officinalis*), which was known as Jamaica pepper in the eighteenth century. Brears gives a recipe for 'pepper cake' dating from 1792 which includes both allspice and ginger. Otherwise, the history of this speciality of the Lake District remains obscure. The present-day version contains black pepper, and this is given in 2 recipes from the 1970s. There is no evidence of a long-standing tradition of the use of this spice in sweet dishes in Cumbria, and it seems probable that modern practice is due to confusion over meanings.

TECHNIQUE:

The ingredients of a commercial pepper cake are listed as wheat flour, raisins, vegetable margarine, eggs, sugar syrup, sugar, mixed candied peel, milk, honey, glucose, oranges, raising agents E334 & E500, black pepper, cloves, and ground ginger. Domestic recipes show flour, treacle, sugar and butter used in the proportions 4:2:2:1. The cake is kept for at least a week before cutting.

REGION OF PRODUCTION:

North West England, Cumbria.

Ormskirk Gingerbread

DESCRIPTION:

A CIRCULAR BISCUIT, ABOUT 60MM DIAMETER, 5MM THICK. WEIGHT: ABOUT 14G. COLOUR: RICH, EVEN BROWN. FLAVOUR AND TEXTURE: SWEET, STRONGLY SPICED WITH GINGER AND OTHER SPICES; CRISP.

HISTORY:

Ormskirk has been noted for gingerbread for at least 200 years. Travellers recorded how the vendors descended upon arriving stage coaches; later, they congregated on the railway station and sold gingerbread to passengers (Hallam, 1979). The only commercial recipe which survived into the late twentieth century is the property of the Mawdsley family who started making the gingerbread in 1800 (Spicer, 1949). For a few years during the 1980s, it went out of commercial production, but has recently been revived and is now made under licence for a grocer in the town.

TECHNIQUE:

The commercial recipe is a trade secret. Several recipes have been published before. They call for flour, butter and soft brown sugar in the proportions 5:2:2. The butter and sugar are creamed, mixed with molasses/Golden Syrup, lemon zest, ginger, cinnamon and flour. This is rolled and cut in rounds. The biscuits are baked at 170°C for 25–30 minutes in falling heat.

REGION OF PRODUCTION:

NORTH WEST ENGLAND, ORMSKIRK (LANCASHIRE).

Blackpool Rock

DESCRIPTION:

CYLINDERS OF PULLED SUGAR, 2–5CM DIAMETER, 20–40CM LONG. COLOUR: A WHITE CENTRE SURROUNDED BY A THIN, PINK OUTER LAYER, WITH LETTERS FORMED OF RED SUGAR RUNNING THE INTERNAL LENGTH OF THE STICK IS TRADITIONAL, BUT YELLOW, ORANGE OR GREEN ARE SOMETIMES USED IN PLACE OF THIS. VARIETIES WITH A STRIPED

OUTSIDE LAYER ARE ALSO MADE. FLAVOUR: USUALLY MINT. COMPOSITION: SUGAR, GLUCOSE, FLAVOURING, COLOUR.

HISTORY:

Seaside rock developed from the art of boiling and pulling sugar. The technique of pulling sugar is used to make other types of rock, with lettering, abstract patterns or pictures of fruit running through it. Some have flavourings of fruit, aniseed or liquorice instead of the old standby, mint. Many miniatures and novelties are also made from pulled sugar, often imitating foods such as fruits, cakes, fish and chips, or bacon and eggs. This visual tradition descends from the delight in sugary imitations made for the sweet banquets of the sixteenth and seventeenth centuries.

The craft of pulled sugar developed into a complex art during the nineteenth century, when confectioners worked out how to recombine batches of differently coloured boiled and pulled sugars into stripes, letters and patterns. A recipe given in the 1830s for striping pulled sugar comes from a Nottingham confectioner, S.W. Stavely, who gave instructions for making Paradise Twist to be streaked red and white. In the middle of the century, Henry Mayhew noted a vendor on the streets of London who had found a method for inserting mottoes into sugar sticks. This is doubtless the precursor of seaside rock – the perfect edible souvenir. The making of rock goes hand in hand with the growth of mass transport and holidays for the working population of industrial England. Blackpool, one of the first beneficiaries of the process, is a natural candidate for particular association with the sweetmeat.

Two people have claims to be the first to market the novelty. One, 'Dynamite Dan', is said to have worked in Morecambe, near Blackpool, in the 1890s. The other, Ben Bullock, was a confectioner from Dewsbury in South Yorkshire. Margaret Race (1990) claims that Bullock began making rock in Dewsbury for sale at Blackpool in the late 1880s, though rock was not made in Blackpool itself until the early twentieth century.

TECHNIQUE:

Sugar, glucose and water are mixed, brought to the boil and allowed to cook to 138°C. The sugar is then poured on to a greased, water-cooled steel table. As it begins to cool, the batch is turned sides-to-middle several times before division into 3. One piece is left plain and the other 2 are coloured: red for the sugar to be used for letters, and pink for that destined for the outer layer. The uncoloured part of the batch is pulled by machine until opaque and white; flavouring is added during this process. Pulling may be done by hand: hanging the cooling sugar on a fixed hook and working it by repeated stretching and folding. This converts the batch into an opaque white mass.

The letters that are destined to run through each stick of rock are formed by making long strips of red sugar, and packing the spaces between them with white. For instance, an 'O' is made from a long cylinder of white sugar, wrapped in a thin layer of red. The form of the letter is only apparent in cross-section. The letters are assembled in the correct order, separated by strips of white. Then a large piece of white sugar is prepared to become the core, and 2 thinner 'flaps'. The rock is assembled by covering the letters reading BLACKPOOL with one flap, and those reading ROCK with the other; the flaps, carrying the letters, are then wrapped around the central core. Then the whole is enclosed in a layer of pink. The entire assemblage is very large at this stage, about 1.5 metres long, 300mm diameter at one end, tapering to about 120mm at the other. The confection is transferred to a batch roller, a machine which maintains it at the correct heat. It rolls it first in one direction and then the other (so that the letters do not twist). Then it is spun, by leading the thinner end of the rock through a narrow aperture and pulling it out in a 'string' on a long table. Once the end of the table is reached, the string is cut and another one begun. As soon as the strings of rock are spun, they must be rolled back and forth by hand until they are completely cool, otherwise, the side closest to the table flattens. The rock is cut into lengths and wrapped in Cellophane.

REGION OF PRODUCTION:

North West England.

Cough Candy

DESCRIPTION:

Cough candy is broken into cubes of roughly 10mm and sold by weight. Colour: light brown, usually with some sugar crystals showing. Flavour: sweet, powerfully herbal, with aniseed, liquorice and horehound. Composition: sugar, herbal essences.

HISTORY:

Cough candy is a survivor of a long tradition of herbal cures. These remedies were made by adding decoctions of herbs to sugar syrups. The latter acted as preservatives and helped to make the bitter flavours more palatable. They were made at home or by apothecaries and sweet-sellers. Stavely (1830) gave a recipe for horehound cake, a mixture of candied sugar and horehound (*Marrubium vulgare*). Mayhew (1851) mentions the vendors of cough drops in the streets of London. According to Skuse (*c.* 1892), cough candy was made from grained sugar, horehound and oil of aniseed. The London product was unlike that in the rest of the country. It was not a candy but a boiled sweet which was pulled and twisted. This type has disappeared.

As a consequence of advances in medicine and drugs, many formulae went out of use or developed into confectionery with a medicinal emphasis. A few herbalists and confectionery companies still make products which might be regarded as sweets. They are mostly to be found in the north of England, and the products are seen as a local taste, notably consumed by the elderly. Fisherman's Friends (see p.54) may be considered as part of the same tradition.

TECHNIQUE:

Sugar is dissolved in water and boiled to 121°C; the syrup is rubbed against the side of the pan until it begins to cloud; the required herbs, essences and flavourings are stirred in; the mixture is poured on to a warm, oiled slab and allowed to set, after which it is broken up.

REGION OF PRODUCTION:

NORTH WEST ENGLAND.

'Tell me what you eat and I will tell you what you are.'

ANTHELME BRILLAT-SAVARIN

Fisherman's Friends

DESCRIPTION:

AN OVAL LOZENGE 19 X 14 X 4MM. WEIGHT: 1G. FLAVOUR: 3 FLAVOURS ARE MADE –ORIGINAL, ANISEED, AND MENTHOL – EACH PRODUCED IN A SUGAR-BASED OR A SUGAR-FREE VERSION. COMPOSITION: SUGAR, DEXTRIN, GLUCOSE SYRUP, PEPPERMINT OIL (1 PER CENT), EDIBLE GUM, MENTHOL (0.3 PER CENT), COLOURING, CHLOROPHYLLIN.

HISTORY:

Fisherman's Friends are a survival of the patent medicines which flourished in nineteenth-century Britain. The formula was compounded by a pharmacist in the town of Fleetwood, James Lofthouse, and first sold as a liquid medicine in 1865. It was specifically intended to ease the throat ailments suffered by trawlermen working for the local fishing industry. Lofthouse of Fleetwood remains the sole manufacturer and the sweet is a registered trademark. The product remained localized until the 1960s, when the company sought new markets, at first in northern England, then throughout the world. Though first intended for coughs or colds, today it is popular as sugar confectionery. In excess of a billion lozenges are produced per annum.

TECHNIQUE:

The tablets are made by a paste method, mixing sugar and other ingredients with a gum base. The paste is rolled, cut, dried and packed. In the sugar-free varieties, sorbitol replaces the sugar, and the tablets are made by mixing the ingredients as a dry powder which is compressed into small lozenges.

REGION OF PRODUCTION:

North West England, Fleetwood (Lancashire).

Kendal Mint Cake

DESCRIPTION:

An oblong mint candy, 150mm long, 90mm wide, 8mm thick. Weight: 170g. Colour: white or pale brown, depending on sugar used. The surface is marked into squares and has a sparkling appearance. Flavour: very sweet, with a powerful mint flavour; a hard, friable texture. Composition: sugar, mint oil. Versions are made with white or brown sugar; mint cake coated with chocolate is also sold.

HISTORY:

Mint cake is a survival of older sweetmeats which were boiled to set in a crystalline mass. They are described in many texts of the 1700s. In 1868, W. Bowness noted that Barbara Gray's shop in Kendal sold gingerbread and mint cake. In the following year, Joseph Wiper established the first of the 4 companies still making mint cake today. Each is based in the town.

Mint cake was popular with Victorian tourists and, in 1914, was supplied to Shackleton's Polar Expedition. This set its character, still used as a marketing ploy, of an energy-giving food, suitable for mountaineers. Each manufacturer has packaging detailing the various expeditions that have used their particular brand.

TECHNIQUE:

Commercial methods used are secret but cannot be much different to that made at home. Sugar, glucose and water are heated in a copper pan until the sugar dissolves. The mixture is cooked to 116°C. The heat is turned off and peppermint oil added. While hot, the mixture is rubbed against the side of the pan until it grains. An alternative method of encouraging sugar crystals to form is to add a small amount of prepared fondant containing crystals of the right size. The mixture is poured into moulds, then cooled and left overnight to crystallize evenly before unmoulding and packing in parchment or plastic wrappers.

REGION OF PRODUCTION:

NORTH WEST ENGLAND, KENDAL (CUMBRIA).

Tizer

DESCRIPTION:

THIS IS A CARBONATED DRINK OF BOLD ORANGE HUE WITH A SWEET CITRUS FLAVOUR.

HISTORY:

At the beginning of the last century, there was a general push towards the commercialization of bottled drinks that combined both pleasure and health-giving properties. Dandelion and Burdock, Sarsaparilla, and 'black beers' (combined with raisin or lemon flavours) belong to this tradition. When healthcare had to be paid for by the recipient, such tonics and pick-me-ups seemed cheap and alluring preventatives. A number of these soft drinks were developed in the Manchester area in the 1920s. 'Tizer' (a trademark coined from the word 'appetizer') was first made in Manchester in 1924 by the company F. Pickup. The brand was extremely popular in the 1920s and 1930s, and the company controlled a large business empire from their Manchester base.

During the Second World War the formula for Tizer was altered. On the death of the original manufacturer in the early 1970s, the company was acquired by A.G. Barr. The new owners researched the original formula intensively and reinstated it.

TECHNIQUE:

Ingredients are water, sugar, carbon dioxide, citric acid, flavourings, preservative, colours. The flavouring and colouring ingredients are

I don't really care about the history of Scouse – maybe it was the Vikings, maybe a nomadic, non-violent Norwegian tribe looking for the Beatles, or maybe aliens – all I know is I love it. It reminds me of childhood and makes me want to hug my mum. Now, for those of you who've never had the good fortune to scoff down a pan of Scouse, here's the basics: lamb (shoulder these days, but a bit of neck is still a fine thing), spuds, carrots, onion and water or stock. So far all Scousers are happy... But like with all good regional recipes, nobody just does that. For me, I like to add celery, red wine or beer, a splash of tabasco, butter on the spuds, a handful of herbs and sometimes (but please don't tell anyone) a dash of Worcestershire sauce. Oh, and pickled beetroot on the side. The heady smell of Scouse when my mum makes it each time the prodigal returns is enough to make me want to put on my jim-jams, watch Blue Peter and look through my football cards, learning everything about all the Liverpool players. Scouse is the best dish in the world – it warms like nothing else, it should feel like a hug going in and like a lovely duvet once it settles. 'You'll never walk alone.'

Simon Rimmer

BROADCASTER, CHEF AND PROPRIETOR, GREEN'S RESTAURANT, MANCHESTER mixed to make a syrup, which is combined with water and sugar, carbonated and bottled.

REGION OF PRODUCTION:

NORTH WEST ENGLAND, MANCHESTER.

Vimto

DESCRIPTION:

THE CORDIAL IS THE ORIGINAL FORM OF THIS DRINK AND IS SOLD IN BOTTLES OF CHARACTERISTIC SHAPE. IT IS DEEP RUBY RED AND TASTES OF BERRY FRUITS WITH VANILLA AND SPICE UNDERTONES. IT IS FORTIFIED WITH VITAMIN C.

HISTORY:

The history of this cordial is similar to that of Tizer. It, too, was Manchester-based and originated in the early 1900s. The inventor was Noel Nichols, a wholesale druggist and herb importer. The name is short for Vimtonic, to reflect an image of health and vigour. Originally made as a cordial, it was swiftly adapted to become a carbonated drink, and the company appointed agents to bottle it in various towns.

During World War II the formula was altered temporarily, although the original has now been reinstated. The Nichols family still retains a substantial interest. Cordials like this, and flavoured black beers can still be bought from Fitzpatrick's Herbal Health, a herbalist and temperance bar in Lancashire, either to take away or mixed on the premises with hot water, or with soda to make a sparkling drink. Vimto is a trademark.

TECHNIQUE:

The flavouring ingredients are a closely guarded secret. They include raspberry, black currant and grape juices, vanilla, capsicum and horehound. It is available sweetened either with sugar or artificial sweeteners. For the cordial, the flavouring and colouring ingredients are mixed into a syrup. If a long drink is required, this is combined with water, carbonated and bottled.

REGION OF PRODUCTION:

North West England, Manchester.

Pickled Damson

DESCRIPTION:

This pickle is dark red with whole fruit visible. The flavour is sweet-sour, with a distinct, rich plum taste, lightly spiced.

HISTORY:

Damsons, *Prunus institia*, are grown throughout Britain and are especially valued in North-West England, where the Lythe Valley in particular contains many old orchards. It is not clear when the plums were first planted there, but they have been associated with Westmoreland for over 150 years. The *Catalogue of Plums at the National Fruit Trials* (1978) records that a variety known as Blue Violet, local to Westmoreland, was received in 1932. There were several methods for preserving them, including jams and fruit pastes. Another was a pickle in vinegar and sugar. They were the only locally-produced fruit available in sufficient quantity for this type of product, as the area does not support the large orchards and market gardens found in the South-East. Total annual production is probably in the order of hundreds of kilos. It is most likely found on market stalls, for instance those run by the Women's Institute.

TECHNIQUE:

A mixture of spirit or malt vinegar, sugar and spices (cloves and cinnamon) is boiled to make a syrup. Each damson is pricked several times and added to this. They are cooked in the pickle for 10 minutes then potted. Some cooks crack the stones and add the kernels.

REGION OF PRODUCTION:

North West England, Lake District.

Taylor's Original Prepared English Mustard

DESCRIPTION:

TAYLOR'S ORIGINAL IS A SMOOTH PASTE, THE COLOUR YELLOW WITH AN OCHRE TONE, VERY SALTY, AROMATIC, MILDLY PUNGENT, WITH A SLIGHT BITTER UNDERTONE.

HISTORY:

Mustard in Britain has a long history (Man and Weir, 1988). The plant was probably introduced by the Romans and it is often mentioned in English texts about food from the Middle Ages onwards. Over the centuries, methods for making mustard evolved and the location of the industry moved several times. In the sixteenth and seventeenth centuries, Tewkesbury mustard from Gloucestershire was the most famous. It was coarse and included much horseradish. It was compacted into balls which were dried and sent round the country. Users could reconstitute it with wine, vinegar or water. Sir Hugh Plat (1602) noticed that in Venice the mustard seed was ground much more finely, as if it were wheat flour. It could be sold ready to be mixed into a condiment. He suggested the idea be adopted in Britain. Eventually, this happened, although it took another hundred years. The invention is attributed to one Mrs Clements of Durham, who began to grind and sift the seed as Plat advised. She sold the powder all over the country in the early eighteenth century.

In 1830, William Taylor, an apothecary in Newport Pagnell, Buckinghamshire, devised a method for making a ready-mixed mustard paste which had excellent flavour and keeping qualities. Taylor never milled mustard flour. He bought his supplies and the product relies on a specific blend of flours, a unique method of mixing and the use of salt as a preservative. The formula was preserved in his recipe book, and is the first known example of a ready-prepared smooth English mustard. Originally stoneware jars, corked and sealed with wax, were used as containers, but now they are glass. The present owner of Taylor's, Ross Southwell, speculates the product's success may have stemmed from its keeping qualities. It was popular with naval officers, who included it in their private stores; the salty paste, well sealed, resisted damage from sea-water and damp conditions.

The company founded by William Taylor diversified into soft drinks – as did many former apothecaries – and this side became the most important. However, by the 1970s it was unable to resist competition from larger businesses and forced again to rely on mustard. In the late 1980s the firm very nearly went out of business but was rescued as a result of a greater public awareness of characterful British food produce and greater vigour imparted by a new owner.

TECHNIQUE:

The formula and method are trade secrets. Mustard flours are purchased, blended and mixed with water, wheat flour, salt and turmeric. This releases an enzyme and a glycoside, giving pungency. The mixture is heated, using a temperature-gradient sufficient to partly destroy the enzyme, or the flavour is too harsh, but leaving enough undamaged to give character.

REGION OF PRODUCTION:

NORTH WEST ENGLAND.

North England

Dock Pudding

DESCRIPTION:

Dock pudding is a brownish-green purée. Its flavour is salty and spinach-like.

HISTORY:

This spring dish, regarded as a blood purifier, is associated with south Yorkshire and the Lake District, where it is known as Easterledge. It is made from common plants which appear early in the year, and probably aided the health of the population by providing necessary vitamins after a long winter diet of preserved and salted foods. In composition it amounts to a vegetable porridge. Essentially, it is now a poverty food, based on groats (husked, crushed oats) with wild greenery. It is better documented in the Lake District, as early-nineteenth-century tourists to the area found it interesting. Peter Brears (1991) discusses some of these reports. He notes that the herbs used include bistort (*Polygonum bistorta*) nettles, lady's mantle, black currant and raspberry leaves, dandelion, plus onions, chives, cabbage and lettuce. Victorians realised its value for the poorer classes: a recipe for sweet docks with oatmeal was included in Alexis Soyer's *Shilling Cookery for the People* (1856 edition).

Production is now limited and mostly domestic, but it is still made for sale in Calderdale, a valley in the southern Pennines. A dock pudding competition is held in the village of Mytholmroyd (West Yorkshire) every May.

TECHNIQUE:

The vegetable ingredients, principally bistort and nettles, plus other herbs as desired, are assembled, washed and stripped from their stems. The greenery, chopped onion and some seasoning are cooked in water for 20 minutes, then oatmeal is added and the mixture cooked for 20 minutes more. The mixture is strained. At this point, it can be put into a jar or deep frozen. To reheat, it is cut in slices and fried in bacon fat for breakfast. It was used to accompany veal in the Lake District.

REGION OF PRODUCTION:

North England, Calderdale (South Yorkshire).

Rhubarb (Forced)

DESCRIPTION:

Forced rhubarb plant stems are used when about 45cm long and 1–2cm across. Their colour is a fine, bright pink skin covering a white interior, terminating in small lemon yellow leaves. When eaten unaccompanied, it is acid and astringent; however, rhubarb is always eaten cooked and sweetened. Outdoor rhubarb has larger, thicker stems of a deeper red or pale green mottled with deep red; the interior of the stem is green, and the leaves, which grow very large and dark green, are cut off before the rhubarb is sold.

HISTORY:

Rhubarb, of Siberian origin, has been known in Britain since the fifteenth century, when its root was imported and used principally in medicine. The first recipe for the kitchen is dated 1783 and even as late as Mrs Beeton (1861), it was 'comparatively little known till within the last twenty or thirty years, but is now cultivated in almost every British garden'. Two decades later, Vilmorin-Andrieux remarked that its cultivation was 'as yet unpractised on the continent', but was of much importance in Great Britain and North America, drawing attention to the rhubarb beds he had seen in the Surrey area. Garden accounts from Viscount Courtenay's estate at Powderham Castle in Devon in 1819 show rhubarb being grown for Exeter market, thus confirming part of Mrs Beeton's statement; further reinforcement comes from gardeners' manuals. In Thomas Mawe and John Abercrombie's *Every Man his*

Own Gardener (1805 edition) there is no mention of the plant. A century later, in Beeton's *Everyday Gardening*, a dozen varieties are listed, all with names of the time like Prince Albert and Victoria.

Although at first rhubarb recipes made no distinction between forced, early-season rhubarb and the main crop grown in the open air, it was that which was raised under cover with extra heat that captured the imagination and was taken up in West Yorkshire. There was a gap in the calendar of dessert fruit that could usefully be filled by the elegant, forced stalks. 'The first rhubarb of the season is to the digestive tract of winter-logged inner man what a good hot bath with plenty of healing soap is to the outer after a bout with plough and harrow,' wrote the American farmer's daughter Della Lutes (1938).

Rhubarb-growing became important in West Yorkshire as the plant was accepted into the English kitchen. Several factors combined to make it a prime crop in an otherwise agriculturally unpromising area. These include heavy clay soils; a climate which tends to cold early in the autumn providing the necessary conditions for early 'vernalization' (the growers' term for dormancy induced by winter temperatures, essential for forced rhubarb); a suitable annual pattern of rainfall which was also of a low pH (because of pollution from neighbouring industrial towns); the availability of suitable fertilizers; a nearby supply of cheap coal to heat forcing sheds; and excellent transport links to the rest of the country, initially through the railways and subsequently by the road network.

Forced rhubarb production has recently declined. It is labour-intensive with low profit margins. It suffers from an old-fashioned image associated with wartime rationing. It has to compete in a market flooded by imported exotic fruit. It remains important in West Yorkshire because the land is unsuitable for most other crops.

TECHNIQUE:

Most farmers grow their own rootstocks. Rhubarb sets (a major segment of root plus one crown bud) are produced by splitting unforced roots aged at least 2 years old. They are grown at a density of about 24,000 per hectare in ground treated heavily with organic material. In West Yorkshire this was farmyard manure, sewage sludge or 'shoddy' (waste woollen rags provided by the local textile industry). Flower stalks are removed in the summer before forcing. To ensure successful forcing, the roots must be vernalized. Practice had developed to accommodate this requirement; growers now keep temperature charts to deduce the correct time. The roots are lifted from mid-November onwards. They are removed to forcing sheds, stacked into beds on the shed floor, then earth is scattered on top and washed down into the roots with water. The plants are then forced in complete darkness at a constant temperature of 26°C for 4–6 weeks, after which the buds produce long sticks of pink rhubarb. As natural light spoils the colour of the leaves, which is a prime determinant of quality, harvesting is carried out by candlelight which illuminates only the area being worked on at a given time. The stalks are carefully picked by hand. The rhubarb is graded into 'Class 1' or 'seconds' (short, thin or poorly-coloured) and packed into 7kg boxes for sale. The exhausted rootstock is ploughed back into the soil.

REGION OF PRODUCTION:

North England, West Yorkshire, between Leeds, Wakefield and Morley.

Ribston Pippin

DESCRIPTION:

A late-season dessert apple, medium size, round- to oblong-conical. Colour: when ripe, has reddish stripes over gold skin, deep cream flesh. Flavour: rich, aromatic flavour, quite acid.

HISTORY:

The apple takes its name from Ribston Hall, Knaresborough (Yorkshire). It is believed to have been raised in the early 1700s from a pip brought from France by Sir Henry Goodricke. It was esteemed by the Victorians: Dallas (1877) described it as 'the favourite apple of England'. It was grown in gardens and orchards all over the country, and is thought a parent of the Cox's Orange Pippin, now the most important British dessert apple. The Ribston Pippin lost commercial popularity in the early 1900s, but continued to be grown in gardens.

REGION OF PRODUCTION:

NORTH ENGLAND, YORKSHIRE.

Coverdale Cheese

DESCRIPTION:

PRESSED, PASTEURIZED COW'S MILK CHEESE IN TALL, WAXED TRUCKLES SIZED 10CM ROUND, 6.5CM TALL; 12.5CM BY 14CM; 12.5CM BY 15CM; 23CM BY 15CM. WEIGHT: 500G–6KG. THE CHIVE-FLAVOURED VARIANT IS MADE IN WHEELS (3KG ONLY). COLOUR: ALMOST WHITE. FLAVOUR AND TEXTURE: MILD, CREAMY WITH SHARP OVERTONES; A CLOSE TEXTURE.

HISTORY:

Coverdale is on the east side of the Pennines. This is a dales cheese; the common heritage of the group is touched upon on p.112. The recipe for Coverdale was recorded in 1912 by Alfred Rowntree. Local historian Kate Mason recalls his stating that milk collected from farms in Coverdale behaved differently to that from other dales, and that he found that if he wished to make Wensleydale he had to modify the recipe. He established a small dairy at Coverham in Coverdale. Production declined during the 1930s and it was not made for some decades after World War II. It has been revived by a nearby creamery who use the 1912 recipe.

TECHNIQUE:

Coverdale is a dales cheese. Differences in micro-climate and flora give the various cheeses distinctive characteristics which are enhanced by variations in recipe and method. The method for Coverdale is not disclosed by the maker but it is broadly similar to Wensleydale. Vegetable rennet is used.

REGION OF PRODUCTION:

North England, North Yorkshire.

Swaledale Cheese

DESCRIPTION:

Pressed, pasteurized ewe's and cow's milk cheeses, sold in weights of 250g, 500g (for both sheep's milk and cow's milk), 2kg (large sheep's milk), 3kg (large cow's milk), and 1.5kg (for the flavoured cow's milk cheeses). Form: small truckles. Colour: very pale cream. Flavour: fresh, lemony, buttery. The cow's milk cheeses are available smoked, or flavoured with chives and garlic, applemint, or soaked in Old Peculier ale (p. 105-6).

HISTORY:

Swaledale belongs to the dales group of small, sharp-flavoured, softish cheeses. When most of the land about there was owned by the Cistercian monastery of Jervaulx, the valleys were farmed from granges – outlying cells that managed vast flocks of sheep (England's wool was the best in Europe) and herds of cows. Cheeses were made in great number. A monastery could get through tons a year. Many were of sheep's milk. The skills first refined by the monks and their labourers spread to the community at large. We are their inheritors.

Swaledale cheese pursued much the same course as Wensleydale (see below) and suffered as badly as its neighbours in the years 1939–45, when cheese-making was centralized and reduced to 2 basic types. Rance (1982) remarks that some on-farm production survived in the area – several are documented – but the makers were convinced their activity was illegal, so little got to the market-place until interest revived in the 1970s. This encouraged some who had learnt to make cheese from their parents, such as Mrs Longstaff who grew up on one of the most noted farms, to begin once more (Mitchell, 1986). On-farm cheese, however, has not taken root and Swaledale is now produced in moderately large quantities by a creamery in the valley. The cow's milk cheeses are available all year. Those made with sheep's milk tend to be seasonal, from January until late autumn. Protected Designations of Origin have been granted to both sheep's milk and cow's milk versions.

TECHNIQUE:

Much of Swaledale is now thinly populated; sheep and cattle form the mainstay of the local economy, pastured on the herb-rich grassland which flourishes on the underlying limestone and millstone grit.

A recipe for Swaledale cheese, still used in the 1980s, was recorded by Patrick Rance. The milk was taken straight from the cow and renneted without the addition of starter at 32°C and left for an hour. The curd was broken into fine pieces and left for an hour, then the whey was poured off. The curd was put into muslin and hung up to drip for 12 hours. The curd was crumbled fine by hand, salted, and mixed, and turned into fine muslin; it was then moulded and pressed for at least 12 hours. On removal from the press, the cheese was unmoulded, the cloth removed and the cheeses stored in a cool place, turned daily for 3 weeks (soft) or up to several months (for a drier, crumbly cheese).

The milk comes from specified herds and flocks in Swaledale. It is pasteurized before use. Exact details of the method are not disclosed. Swaledale is based on a similar recipe to Wensleydale and both use cow's milk and sheep's milk. The cheeses are lightly pressed, and salted by brining after removal from the moulds.

REGION OF PRODUCTION:

NORTH ENGLAND, NORTH YORKSHIRE.

Wensleydale Cheese

DESCRIPTION:

HARD, PRESSED COW'S MILK CHEESE ONCE INVARIABLY MADE IN SMALL TRUCKLES 16CM DIAMETER AND 18CM HIGH. SIZE NOW DEPENDS ON WEIGHT, WHICH IS 450G–2.3KG. BLOCK VERSIONS ARE ALSO MADE. COLOUR: WHITE; THE BLUE BECOMES A PALE CREAM WITH BLUE VEINS. FLAVOUR AND TEXTURE: A GOOD WENSLEYDALE HAS A MILD SHARP FLAVOUR AND A CRUMBLY, MOIST CURD. A SOFT EWE'S MILK CHEESE IS ALSO MADE UNDER THE NAME WENSLEYDALE.

HISTORY:

Wensleydale cheese has suffered much from being poorly copied. This is unfortunate, as it has a long and interesting history and is the only British territorial cheese which can clearly be demonstrated to have its origin in a sheep's milk cheese. In the past, it was usually blue-veined, with a moist, spreadable consistency.

Wensleydale is just one of several river valleys cut into the Pennine hills. The predominant rock is limestone. The economy has always been based on pastoral farming; cheese-making may have been carried on from a very early date. Cistercian monks are always claimed to have brought recipes and methods which naturalized to become the true Wensleydale. Cheeses are mentioned in monastic inventories from the twelfth century. The monks may have instructed tenant farmers on their surplus land in the art of cheese-making, the cheese later being used to pay the rent. After the dissolution of the monasteries, the lay population continued to make cheese using a mixture of cow's and sheep's milk. The use of sheep's milk gradually disappeared in Wensleydale although it survived in neighbouring areas.

In the nineteenth century, cheese-making was a seasonal activity, commencing in mid-May. Two shapes were made, those from spring and late autumn being flat millstones and from mid-season being tall truckles. Everything stopped with the first frost. The method used until late in the nineteenth century was based on the use of full-cream milk, with that from the evening's milking being ripened to start the next morning's. The cheeses were usually salted externally, in a brine bath or by brine washing. Much of the cheese blued naturally. The use of the name Wensleydale for the cheese is relatively recent. The first firm date is the first half of the nineteenth century, when cheese fairs began in the local market town of Leyburn.

Factory production commenced in the early 1900s, when farmhouse production was already in decline. Standardization of the recipe, particularly shifting to salting the curd in preference to brine washing, altered the consistency, and a higher proportion was eaten young, reducing the number of blue cheeses. By the 1930s, a local man, Kit Calvert, realizing that Wensleydale made by the old methods was under threat, formed the Wensleydale Cheesemakers Association to aid those farmers still following the practices of their ancestors. In the end, the struggle was too much for them and such cheeses died out in the late 1950s. Attempts at revival after wartime rationing had failed because of inflexible rules imposed by the Milk Marketing Board. It was not until renewed interest in small-scale cheesemaking during the 1980s that farmhouse Wensleydale was seen once more.

Since 1939–45, most Wensleydale has been sold young and only a very limited quantity of blue is available. In Yorkshire, it is traditionally served with fruit cake or apple pie, or eaten with oatcakes. Formerly it was a summer-only cheese, but now is made throughout the year.

TECHNIQUE:

Craft method: the milk is heated to 21°C and a small proportion of starter added. Then the morning milk is mixed in and the temperature raised to 28°C for the addition of rennet. The surface is stirred gently to prevent the cream from rising. The curd is cut into 3mm cubes and then settled for 10 minutes before cutting again; then it is settled for 20 minutes, followed by 20 minutes' stirring as the temperature rises to 30°C; the curd is then left in the whey for up to an hour. It is drained and milled into walnut-sized pieces. Salt may be added before or after this process. The cheese is packed into cloth-lined moulds; the following day they are turned, lightly weighted for 24 hours, then turned again. They are washed in salt water and bandaged. Wensleydale cheese is eaten after maturing for between 2 weeks and 3 months.

In the creamery method the temperatures are slightly higher. Blue Wensleydale requires a less acid, softer curd, more coarsely milled and lightly pressed. An even temperature of 12°C and a humidity of 95 per cent is needed during the ripening; the cheese may be inoculated with the mould spores and pierced with needles during ripening to encourage blueing.

REGION OF PRODUCTION:

North England, North Yorkshire.

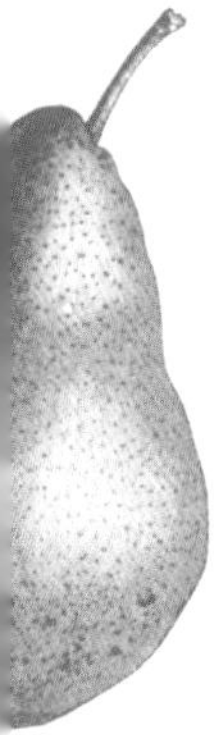

Denby Dale Pie

DESCRIPTION:

An oblong, cooked meat and potato pie. Small pies made in the village are 9cm long, 5cm wide, 3cm deep, weighing 175g. Colour: pale gold pastry covering pale potato layer with browned beef filling. Flavour: savoury beef.

HISTORY:

The Denby Dale is a special-occasion pie baked in the West Riding village of that name once in about every 25 years; the last making took place in 2000. Large celebration pies have been recorded elsewhere in England, but it is its huge size which distinguishes the Denby Dale (Bostwick, 1987). Custom has it that each time the pie is baked, it should be larger than the last. That baked in 2000 weighed 12 tonnes and measured 40 foot long.

The first to be documented was in 1788 to celebrate the return to health of King George III. This was followed by: the Victory Pie (1815, to commemorate the Battle of Waterloo); the Repeal of the Corn Laws Pie (1846, to celebrate the removal of unpopular legislation which kept the price of corn artificially high); the Golden Jubilee Pie (27 August 1887, intended to celebrate Queen Victoria's Golden Jubilee); the Resurrection Pie (3 September 1887, to replace the Golden Jubilee Pie which went bad and had to be buried in quicklime); the Repeal of the Corn Laws Jubilee Pie (1896, commemorating that from 50 years earlier); the Infirmary Pie (1928, to raise funds for the local hospital); the Would-Be Coronation Pie (1953, planned but never made, because meat was still rationed in the aftermath of the Second World War); the Village Hall Pie (1964, to raise funds for a community hall); the Bicentenary Pie (1988, to recall the beginning of the tradition); and, most recently, the Millennium Pie (2000, to celebrate the new Millennium and the Queen Mother's 100th birthday). A local butcher holds the formula for a special seasoning mixture which has been used in the last 2 pies and is also put into small pies made from day to day.

The pie was originally filled with meat and game, but after the débâcle of 1887, the recipe was changed to one similar to that now used. This is a gigantic version of the common meat and potato pie, a stew of beef covered with sliced potato, topped with shortcrust pastry and baked. These pies are well known in Yorkshire and Lancashire. Fresh beef is always used, distinguishing them from cottage pies, which are leftover meat, and demonstrating a relationship with Lancashire hotpot, a mutton stew covered with sliced potatoes. Small meat and potato pies are popular for dinner in the industrial areas of West Yorkshire and South Lancashire. Only the village of Denby Dale makes the huge pies.

TECHNIQUE:

The last Denby Dale Pie to be baked entire was in 1928. To satisfy hygiene regulations, large pies are now made by producing a stew of beef and potato using the special seasoning, cooking the crust separately and assembling on site.

Small pies are made as follows. The meat is always fresh beef, cut into pieces of 1–2cm and partially cooked with seasoning and liquid (usually water) to produce plenty of gravy. The beef is first covered with a layer of sliced, lightly seasoned raw potato, then with a sheet of short-crust and baked for 45 minutes, at 190°C.

REGION OF PRODUCTION:

NORTH ENGLAND, WEST YORKSHIRE AND SOUTH LANCASHIRE.

Elder

DESCRIPTION:

Cooked cow's udder. Colour: pink, mottled with creamy-yellow. Flavour: a little like tongue, but blander, with a chewy texture.

HISTORY:

Elder is a dialect word for cow's udder known in much of the north and west of Britain, but now archaic except in parts of Yorkshire and Lancashire. The use of udder as food is not well-documented, but was formerly widespread. When the pig-cook Ursula was bantering with her friend Knockem in Jonson's *Bartholomew Fair* (1614), she denies reports of her demise of a surfeit of bottle-ale and tripes. 'No,' replied Knockem, 'it was better meat, it was cow's udders.' Today, its sale is limited to the industrial towns of South-West Yorkshire and East Lancashire (Brown, 1987). The first recorded use of the word elder appears to be in a collection of North-Country dialect published in the late 1600s. Presented as thick slices, arranged on trays in the windows of cooked meat shops and takeaway food shops, elder has a very distinctive appearance, mostly due to the colour. The texture is also particular, resembling coarse-textured, chewy tongue. Martha Bradley (1756) counselled that it should treated in exactly the same way as tongue. In northern towns and villages, it is customarily eaten cold with salt and malt vinegar, but there are many more interesting ways of dealing with it should this food ever return to popularity.

TECHNIQUE:

The udder is skinned and drained of any remaining milk. It is boiled for about 6 hours (sometimes more) until tender; the elder is left to cool in the liquid, and may be given a second boiling for another 2 hours the next day, then rapidly cooled. It is given a final dressing to remove excess fat and scraps of skin, then trimmed neatly.

REGION OF PRODUCTION:

North England, South West Yorkshire, East Lancashire.

Middle White Pig

DESCRIPTION:

A dressed carcass of 50kg at 12–16 weeks. A short, deep body, rounded hams and distinctive snub nose. A traditionally-reared Middle White yields darker lean than commercial breeds; it is well-marbled, tender, juicy, with excellent flavour; a breed which is good as sucking pig.

HISTORY:

As the name suggests, there are other white pigs: the Large White is still important commercially and it is thought there was also a Small White, now vanished. They flourished in Yorkshire during the late eighteenth and early nineteenth centuries when, as detailed by William Youatt, the breeding of prize pigs on a small scale was both a hobby and a source of meat and income for craftsmen and cottagers (Samuel, 1860). The Middle White may have originated in a cross between the Small White and an imported Chinese pig, to give the characteristic snub profile and rounded shape. An early name was the Yorkshire. Until World War II, they were a popular pork breed but subsequently declined in numbers because tastes in meat changed.

TECHNIQUE:

Middle Whites can be kept outdoors, at least in the summer, but do not forage as efficiently as other breeds because of their short noses. Most people keep them as sty pigs, with food entirely provided. This was the method used by cottagers and small farmers, who had limited space but none the less access to domestic and garden waste or edible by-products such as spent grain from brewing. For sucking pig, they are killed at 7–8 weeks; for pork they are grown on to 12–16 weeks. To obtain pork suitable for the current market this breed should be slaughtered before it accumulates large amounts of fat.

REGION OF PRODUCTION:

North England.

Polony

DESCRIPTION:

A COOKED PORK SAUSAGE SOLD IN LOOPS 40–50CM LONG; ABOUT 4CM DIAMETER. COLOUR: THE SKIN IS BRIGHT RED, ENCLOSING PALE PINK MEAT. FLAVOUR: MILD CURED-PORK FLAVOUR, LIGHTLY SPICED AND SMOKED.

HISTORY:

The name may be a corruption of Polonia (Poland) or Bologna, the Italian town. Opinion tends towards the latter. Whichever, polony has had over 300 years to develop a British identity, for Bologna or Polony sausage was popular in the seventeenth century (Wilson, 1973). A recipe for 'Bolonia' sausages in John Nott (1726) displays several characteristics still associated with polony, including a flour paste to bind, large size, and the fact that they were pre-cooked. Polony has always been red; red sage, saltpetre, red wine or cochineal were all used as colourings.

The spa town of Bath, close to an important pig-raising area, was famous for polony in the past. Smith (1951) mentions Bath polonies, which 'have been given a high place amongst those eatables for which the city has become famous', and mentions Dill's Polonies, Cheap Street, in existence since 1784 (they have now vanished). The second area linked with them was Yorkshire. Douglas's *Encyclopaedia* gave a Yorkshire recipe including pork and rice or rusk plus salt, white pepper, cayenne, nutmeg and mace. *Law's Grocer's Manual* (*c.* 1895) stated that 'Sheffield is more celebrated for these cooked sausages than any other town in England.' Finney's instructions for pork butchers included 2 named polony mixtures – Yorkshire and Bath – but all the others were identified only by number (1915). In the 1930s, Sheffield polony was among butcher's recipes published by Percy Dalton. It included lean pork, mutton or corned beef, ham or beef fat, flour and rusk, salt, pepper, mace, coriander and ginger. It is difficult to escape the conclusion that individual butchers used whatever ingredients they felt would achieve the correct texture.

Polonies still flourish and many butchers make their own. Highly commercialized polony in a red plastic skin is sold in supermarkets, but bears little resemblance to good artisan versions.

TECHNIQUE:

A mixture of lean and fat raw pork is chopped fine, mixed with flour paste or rusk and seasonings according to individual recipes (salt, pepper, mace, coriander and ginger are all cited), then filled into wide casings. They are boiled for about 45 minutes with red food colouring in the water. They are chilled in iced water, drained and displayed for sale and are sold by weight.

REGION OF PRODUCTION:

NORTH ENGLAND, YORKSHIRE.

York Ham

DESCRIPTION:

A CURED HAM. WEIGHT: ABOUT 14KG. COLOUR: PALE GOLD OR BROWN RIND, WHITE FAT AND DEEP RED LEAN WHEN UNCOOKED; ROSE-PINK LEAN AFTER COOKING. FLAVOUR: RICH SALTY HAM, WITH DISTINCT PORK FLAVOUR, DRY TEXTURE.

HISTORY:

York hams are esteemed far beyond English shores. There are countless foreign references to them. Take Flaubert's *Education Sentimentale* (1869), describing a dinner given by the dandified Vicomte de Cisy: 'For the first course alone, there was a sturgeon's head drenched in champagne, a York ham cooked in tokay, thrushes *au gratin*, roast quail, a *vol-au-vent Béchamel*, a *sauté* of red-legged partridges, and, flanking all this, stringed potatoes mixed with truffles.' York ham kept high-falutin' company. But curiously little attention was ever paid to the delicacy in the place whence it takes its name. There are several reasons why this might be. Firstly, it would probably be more accurate to regard them as hams from the county rather than the city of York. In 1747, the earliest mention found so far, Hannah

Glasse wrote 'Yorkshire is famous for Hams'. She thought it was the quality of the salt used in their manufacture which made the difference. William Ellis, at about the same time, noticed the London market being flooded by cheap Yorkshire ham. By 1817 they had become known as 'York Hams'; Kitchiner said that 'real' York hams were preferable to any, but gave no reasons. The word suggests that imitations were known and the term was becoming generic, implying a particular cure not a place of birth.

Douglas's *Encyclopaedia* (*c.* 1905) described hams cured in Ireland for export to France as 'York' hams: they were small, 12lb (6kg) in weight, mildly cured and lightly smoked, whereas Yorkshire-produced hams were large, up to 50lb (25kg), and were very salty.

Opinions vary as to whether York (or Yorkshire) hams should be smoked. The *Magazine of Domestic Economy* (1838) said they were smoked over wood shavings with aromatic herbs. It has been claimed by various twentieth-century authors (for instance Hartley, 1954) that York hams were made in the Middle Ages, and smoked over sawdust generated from building the cathedral in the town. There is no evidence for this. Scott's, the butchers in York who produce them today, do not smoke them. In the past, the quality of the pigs – Yorkshire was the home of the Large White, an important commercial breed – may well have contributed to the excellence of hams from Yorkshire, just as did the availability of feed, which included spent brewers' grain. The growth of river and canal transport links may also have been a factor in the low price of York ham in the eighteenth century. Modern York hams are smaller, about 14kg, and less salty.

TECHNIQUE:

The pork legs, cut from bacon pigs, must carry a specified level of fat, otherwise they become dry; they are long-cut, giving a rounded shape. They are cured in dry salt with saltpetre and sugar for 1 month, then drained for 3 days and matured for 4–24 months, depending on the manufacturer. Temperature and humidity are controlled, leading to a shorter maturing time as well as production all year round. W. Hogan

(1978) remarked that long and careful maturing, over 6 months, was the true secret of a modern York ham.

REGION OF PRODUCTION:

North England, Yorkshire.

Fat Rascal

DESCRIPTION:

A round, domed teacake about 100mm diameter, 30–40mm deep. Weight: about 170g. Colour and texture: rich brown crust, cracked in places with paler, less highly baked inside showing through; close-textured, pale yellow inside, with currants and candied peel. Flavour: sweetish with citrus note.

HISTORY:

The origin of the name for these teacakes is unknown, but has been in use since at least the mid-nineteenth century; a reference from the 1860s makes clear that the cake was composed of flour, currants and butter or cream, and that it was closely associated with the Cleveland area, on the borders of Durham and Yorkshire. It was not a complex dough. It was raised with baking soda and was easy for domestic cooks to bake in a 'yetling' or pot oven, a cast iron, deep, lidded pot raised on short legs which could be placed in hot ashes in the fireplace. There are several North-Country cakes of this nature with more or less evocative names such as girdle cake, flap cake or turf cake. Singin' hinnies, made in Durham and Northumberland, are based on a similar recipe, as are rock buns. White (1932) and Brears (1987) cite variations, for example using lard instead of butter.

Fat rascals from bakers' shops are larger and richer than those which are made at home; they are baked in an oven, and have an added decoration of a face made from halved glacé cherries and almonds which is not associated with the cakes of the past. Modern versions are usually leavened with baking powder.

TECHNIQUE:

The ratio of flour to fat is 2:1. The dough is rolled out to a sheet a little over a centimetre thick and cut into rounds of about 60mm across. They are baked for 10–15 minutes at about 200°C.

REGION OF PRODUCTION:

NORTH ENGLAND, YORKSHIRE.

Muffin

DESCRIPTION:

CIRCULAR FLAT BREAD, 80–90MM DIAMETER, 30MM DEEP. WEIGHT: ABOUT 70G. COLOUR: PALE GOLD OR WHITE; ALMOST WHITE AROUND THE SIDES. SOFT TEXTURE, ALWAYS EATEN TOASTED.

HISTORY:

Muffins are food for English tea. Their history, and that of crumpets which are closely related, is confusing. The term is first recorded in English during the early eighteenth century. The *OED* suggests it is 'a word connected with old French *moufflet*, soft, said of bread'. The characteristics of softness and a flat shape, usually baked on a hot stone or griddle, are essential points. However, a firm definition of early muffins or crumpets is elusive (David, 1977). Peter Brears (1984) cites a seventeenth-century Yorkshire recipe for oatcakes which in fact contains no oats and would have turned out like a muffin. A recipe for muffins from Hannah Glasse (1747) is for soft flat cakes of plain yeast-leavened dough. (She instructed the consumer to pull, not cut the muffin: a *sine qua non* of muffin consumption in the years since her book.) Recipes over the following 150 years varied in terms of relative richness, some included eggs, butter or milk. The results were always cooked on hearthstones or iron plates and, according to *Law's Grocer's Manual*, bakers had special stones set in brick for the purpose.

The chief distinction between muffins and crumpets is the consistency of the raw mixture. A muffin is made with a soft dough while crumpets use a pouring batter. The flour preferred for muffins was usually stronger (with more protein) than that for crumpets.

For years muffins were cried through the streets of cities by vendors who bought their stock from bakers. The breads were folded in flannel to keep hot. They appear to have been eaten for tea by almost everyone. Housewives bought them from the muffin men, gentlemen's clubs served them for tea in silver dishes, and famous writers made observations about them. Early in the twentieth century, their popularity declined, the muffin man vanished, the breads themselves a rarity. The one area where they survived was Lancashire and West Yorkshire. This is a stronghold of griddle-baking, and Joseph Wright (1896–1905) recorded the word muffin as Lancashire and Yorkshire dialect. Whether this represents some deeper tradition is not clear, but David Mabey (1978) commented that muffins were rarely seen except in Lancashire, where they were still being made and sold by bakers when he was writing.

Matters have changed much since then. The muffin has been adopted by supermarkets and plant bakers, who fill it with dried fruit or spices for variation's sake. The modern muffin has come to be (mostly because of these extra ingredients) a rather close-textured bread cake, but some craft bakers make very good muffins of the old type; one company in Lancashire uses a local recipe which dates back at least 70 years.

The English muffin is quite different from the American, which is a chemically-leavened bun or cake with or without added flavouring. English muffins are eaten by toasting on the outside, split by pulling apart, and buttered by laying on a piece of butter. The halves are then put back together and kept warm until the butter has melted. They are eaten for tea, but now often for breakfast as well.

TECHNIQUE:

For muffin making, the texture of the dough and the heat of the griddle are vital. These can only be learnt through experience. The craft method needs a soft dough made from warmed flour, water, yeast, salt, and small quantities of sugar and butter. The butter is rubbed through the dry ingredients; the yeast is dispersed in the water, and used to mix the dough. It is left to rise for 1 hour, then knocked back, scaled off and shaped into rounds. These are placed on trays dusted with rice flour and proved. The rounds are placed in hoops on a hot-plate; halfway through cooking they are turned over.

REGION OF PRODUCTION:

NORTH ENGLAND, LANCASHIRE, WEST YORKSHIRE.

Ripon Spice Cake

DESCRIPTION:

A LOAF 140MM LONG, 70MM WIDE, 90MM HIGH. WEIGHT: ABOUT 450G. COLOUR: RICH BROWN CRUST, BEIGE CRUMB WITH PROMINENT FRUIT. FLAVOUR: SWEET, AROMATIC, HEAVILY SPICED.

HISTORY:

No early references have been found to substantiate a long association of this cake with Ripon. Spice cakes, however, were known in the region and made frequently until at least 1939–45. They were a Christmas speciality and known as Yule spice cakes. Recipes show them containing sugar, dried fruit, and candied peel, enriched with butter and lard and flavoured with nutmeg and lemon. Cassell's *Dictionary of Cookery* (1896) includes an entry under the heading 'Yorkshire Spice Cake (sometimes called Yule Cake)'. It points to several other recipes which it would classify together, including 'Aunt Edward's Christmas Cake', remarking that the Yorkshire cake was 'freely offered to strangers and presented to friends, and frequently eaten with cheese instead of bread'.

Today's recipe belongs to the Ripon business which produces the cake. It was bought with the shop 20 years ago. It deserves attention because it contains elements which are old – the use of lard as a shortening and yeast as a leavening agent – alongside candied cherries and walnuts which are both relatively new to the British cake-baking tradition. If the Yule spice cakes used to be made for Christmas, the present maker ignores that feast, leaves Yule out of the name altogether and concentrates production on the Ripon festival of St Wilfrid's (see Wilfra cakes, below). This is an innovation. There is but the one maker of Ripon spice cakes but Yule spice cakes can still sometimes be bought from bakeries in North Yorkshire.

TECHNIQUE:

The cake is a lightly sweetened, yeast-leavened cake. Once enriched with lard, changes in taste have led to its replacement by margarine. Some recipes also called for eggs. Dried fruit, candied cherries, walnuts and spices, including cinnamon and nutmeg, are added and kneaded through. The mixture is scaled off, placed in tins and proved. They are baked at 150–160°C for 60–90 minutes. The cakes are dusted with icing sugar before going on sale.

REGION OF PRODUCTION:

North England, Ripon (North Yorkshire).

Suet Cake

DESCRIPTION:

Circular biscuits or cakes, 80mm diameter, 10mm thick. Weight: 75g. Colour: pale gold, flecked with dried fruit. Flavour and texture: bland and plain.

HISTORY:

Suet cakes are one representative of a group of bland, close-textured, pastry-type biscuits made in West Yorkshire and East Lancashire. They are now considered old-fashioned and production is limited but the spread of recipes and names suggests they were formerly common. Variants include hard cakes, fatty cakes (West Riding of Yorkshire), sad cakes (West Riding of Yorkshire, Rossendale area of Lancashire) and cracknells (Blackburn). The descriptor 'sad' indicates a baked item which does not rise very much, while 'hard cakes' suggests the texture. Brears (1987) gives some details: fatty cake is a short cake of flour with butter, dripping or lard; sad cakes are made from a flour and lard dough leavened with baking powder and filled with currants and a little sugar;

suet cakes are made from flour shortened with lard, suet, currants and yeast. These were cooked on a bakstone, the regional term and spelling for griddle.

Boyd (1988) shows Blackburn cracknells to be biscuits of the same type but without the fruit. Cracknell is a word descended from the French *craquelin*, which described 2 sorts of dry cake or biscuit. The first was a dough poached then dried in the oven, described by Dawson (1596), the second was a plain, sugared biscuit for which recipes abound. Citations of the other names have not been found before 1850, but this is not conclusive. They are probably ancient in origin. The use of the word cake to indicate pastry or biscuits is very old. The use of currants in the mixture relates them to other pastries popular in the area, such as Eccles cakes and Chorley cakes. So far, one baker has been located making suet cakes (a family-owned business, founded about a century ago), and one other which bakes Blackburn cracknells. Several early references relate these cakes specifically to breakfast. They are usually spread with butter.

TECHNIQUE:

Suet cakes were originally leavened with yeast. The lard was rubbed into the flour, the other ingredients added and some yeast, mixed with milk and water, used to form a dough. This was shaped into small cakes, proved and baked. Those made now are leavened with baking powder. They require flour, suet, lard and currants in the proportions 4:1:1:1. A firm dough is rolled to 10mm thick, cut into cakes and baked at 170°C until pale gold.

Sad cakes are a short pastry (flour and fat in the proportions 2:1), mixed with currants and rolled out. According to Mabey (1978) they varied from a type of pasty in which the currants were kept in the middle of a pastry envelope, to something more like a biscuit, with the currants thoroughly incorporated into thin pastry. Spicer (1949) mentions these, and directs the cook to cut them into fancy shapes.

A Yorkshire recipe for hard cakes is for plain biscuits with no currants, raised with volatile salts – ammonium carbonate (White, 1932).

REGION OF PRODUCTION:

North England, Yorkshire–Lancashire border.

Wilfra Tart

DESCRIPTION:

A double-crust pie with a decoration of 3 pastry leaves around a central vent, 120–130mm diameter, 20mm deep. Weight: about 350g. Colour: pale gold pastry, with yellow melted cheese showing through the central hole. Flavour: crisp unsweetened pastry, with a filling of sweetened apple and a layer of cheese.

HISTORY:

Various tarts have been known by this name in the past, with fillings such as sweet mincemeat, curd cheese, and jam. That described here is the one commercially available today.

Wilfra tarts are made in the town of Ripon in North Yorkshire. The name is a corruption of St Wilfrid (634–709, bishop of York and monk at Ripon), the patron of the town's cathedral. The tarts are made for a procession held in his honour on the Saturday before the first Monday in August. This procession has a history which stretches back at least to the late Middle Ages. Earlier evidence about the tarts themselves is not forthcoming. Hence the first description is in White (1932) who noted them as small jam tarts or cheesecakes. Later sources comment that the tarts were handed out to passers-by or left on plates by house doorways for people to help themselves.

At least 2 versions now seem to be known; the apple and cheese version made for sale, and another recipe which calls for a filling of butter, ground almonds, sugar, lemon rind, soaked breadcrumbs and egg. This last is similar to early almond cheesecake recipes, for instance Eliza Smith's (1758). The origin of the apple and cheese combination is less obvious. English cooks were rather indiscriminate about the basis of their cheesecakes, which quite often contained no cheese or curded milk but were based on eggs and almonds instead; later, ground rice or desiccated coconut were substituted for the almonds, and sometimes mashed potato was added. It is possible that the current recipe is an evolution of a formerly more complex 'cheesecake' which included apples amongst its ingredients. The baker who now bakes it uses a recipe which belonged to the business which he acquired some 25 years ago. He is the only producer.

TECHNIQUE:

An English shortcrust is used to line a deep pie dish, and a portion is rolled out for the top. A layer of sliced apples is placed in the bottom, brown sugar sprinkled over, and some grated cheese placed on top. This should traditionally be Wensleydale but Cheddar, which is a deeper yellow, is used in preference. The pie is covered and decorated. It is baked at 180°C for about 40 minutes. It may be eaten hot or cold.

REGION OF PRODUCTION:

North England, Ripon (North Yorkshire).

Whitby Gingerbread

DESCRIPTION:

A loaf, with a pattern of lozenges imprinted on the surface, 140mm long, 90mm wide, 60mm deep. Weight: about 500g. Colour: chestnut brown. Flavour and texture: mildly spiced, dry.

HISTORY:

Whitby is a small port on the Yorkshire coast. Tradition has it that gingerbread has been made there since the 1700s. It was certainly known by the time the company which now makes it, Elizabeth Botham & Sons, was established in 1865. According to Joe Botham, who now runs the company, references are found in the *Whitby Gazette* for 'gingerbread for ships' during the 1850s. He speculates that this trade was the reason for the characteristically dry texture and excellent keeping-qualities of the cake. Recipe and method show links with the oatmeal-based parkin known further west. Originally the gingerbread was baked in blocks of

4lb (1.8kg) which were then quartered. The loaves are now cut into thin slices, spread with butter, and eaten with the mild cheeses produced in the Yorkshire Dales. It was a customary food at Christmas.

TECHNIQUE:

The exact method is a trade secret but the gingerbread uses lard which is melted with a dark syrup. Flour, spices, a powder raising agent, water and other ingredients are mixed to make a very sticky dough. After a period of resting, this is scaled off, shaped, placed in tins, marked with a mould, and given a long bake in gentle heat. The gingerbread is then matured for several weeks before sale.

REGION OF PRODUCTION:

North-East England, Whitby (North Yorkshire).

Whitby Lemon Bun

DESCRIPTION:

A square or round bun, deep in proportion to height, with a thickly iced top; about 100mm diameter, 50mm high. Weight: 70–80g. Colour: gold-brown crust on top, pale underside, torn appearance on sides, where buns are torn apart after baking; white icing; cream-yellow crumb when cut, with dried fruit. Flavour: slightly sweetened and enriched bread, light, soft open texture, lemon-flavoured icing.

HISTORY:

According to Joe Botham, who makes these buns in Whitby, no one is sure why they became a speciality of the town, except that they appear to have been one of the original lines made by Mrs Elizabeth Botham, who founded the bakery that bears her name in 1864. The dough is similar in taste to that used for other nineteenth-century enriched breads; this is a local version. It is richer than the small teacakes commonly made in Yorkshire, yet not as rich as the 'twopenny buns' recorded in a late eighteenth-century manuscript from the hills to the west of Whitby.

Whitby is a fishing port and developed as a popular tourist resort in the 1800s. Perhaps this had something to do with the success of the buns. It would inevitably bring a demand for foods that visitors found interesting and acceptable. The same imperative governing local specialities is seen in Bath buns, Bath Olivers and Sally Lunns. In the 1940s, the former manager of Botham's in Whitby (a descendant of the founder) moved to the city of Leeds and began to make his own version. It is slightly drier, less sweet, and baked as an individual bun (rather than in a batch torn asunder after baking). Only these 2 companies have been identified as making the buns.

TECHNIQUE:

The exact recipe is a trade secret. The buns are based on a soft, rich dough similar to that used for the Sally Lunn. The mixture is yeast-leavened, and sultanas are kneaded in; the dough is scaled off, shaped, placed close together on trays and 'batch baked': as the dough rises, the individual buns are so close together that they touch and have to be pulled apart on removal from the oven. When cooled, they are given a thick cap of lemon-flavoured glacé icing.

REGION OF PRODUCTION:

North England, Yorkshire.

Yorkshire Curd Tart

DESCRIPTION:

A circular open tart, a common size is 140mm wide, 20mm deep; individual curd tarts are not customary. Weight: one of the size quoted weighs approximately 220g. Colour: the pastry shell bakes to a pale gold; the filling has a granular appearance which colours unevenly from cream to golden brown; it is speckled with currants. Flavour and texture: mild, creamy and sweet, with granulated texture.

HISTORY:

A curd tart is also known as a cheesecake. Baked cheesecakes have been known in England since at least the thirteenth century

(Wilson, 1973), when household accounts record 'cheese for tarts' – perhaps referring to hard cheese rather than the fresh cheese used in later recipes. An early recipe, essentially the same as that used today, including both currants and nutmeg, is found in Lady Elinor Fettiplace's manuscript (Spurling, 1987). Subsequently, there is an infinity of instructions for curd cheesecakes in published manuals. Similar dishes, which were colloquially called cheesecakes but which contained ground almonds or other ingredients instead of curd to thicken the custard, were also made. What is not clear is the point at which these dishes were given up by the majority of the population and became local specialities. The evidence available suggests this took place some time between 1750 (when both Mrs Raffald and Mrs Smith included recipes for cheesecakes in their books, which were known throughout the country) and 1860 (when neither Miss Acton nor Mrs Beeton did). Nor is it clear why certain areas maintained a habit of making them. Today, curd tarts are now very much local specialities and their stronghold is Yorkshire – specifically for festive times, notably Whitsuntide and Christmas – where once they were gathered from housewives for communal feasts. This tradition is recorded in the towns of Muker and Redmire and in Fulford, now a suburb of York (Brears, 1987). Today, they have few associations with particular events and they are baked commercially by most bakeries in Yorkshire. Curd tarts have also been identified in Lincolnshire.

TECHNIQUE:

The curd is based on cow's milk. Traditionally, colostrum is used; this is simply brought to the boil, at which point it curdles naturally. Modern dairy practice now makes colostrum difficult to obtain. There are several other methods for making curd, including heating milk to just below boiling then stirring in Epsom salts, adding vinegar, adding rennet to warm milk, and stirring fresh, cold buttermilk into ordinary milk heated almost to boiling. The curd is then cooled and strained. Few make their own curd, but those who do have individual recipes which vary in their cream content; some give a very rich result.

The strained curd is mixed with sugar, eggs, margarine or butter and currants. Flavourings include nutmeg, lemon zest or rum. The mixture is beaten to break the curd into small particles. The mixture can be used immediately but it is thought better kept 1–3 days. An unsweetened short-crust pastry using lard is used. The curd mixture is poured on to the uncooked pastry to the desired depth. The tarts are baked at 180°C for about 30 minutes.

REGION OF PRODUCTION:

North England, Yorkshire.

Yorkshire Mint Pasty

DESCRIPTION:

A flat pastry made in large square trays about 20mm deep. When offered for sale, it is cut into pieces 8mm wide, 80mm long. Weight: about 100g per piece. Colour: pale gold pastry, with a dark layer of currants. Flavour: sweet, with dried fruit and mint.

HISTORY:

The large size of a mint pasty relates it to the 'currant slice', made in a similar shape but omitting the mint, which is relatively common in British bakers' shops. The form, consisting of a layer of currants and other ingredients sandwiched between pastry, points to a relationship with regional specialities such as Chorley and Eccles cakes. A 'mint cake' of mint-flavoured pastry is mentioned from the beginning of the nineteenth century in Wright (1896–1905), and Florence White (1932) gives a recipe 'To make Old Yorkshire Mint Pasty', attributed to an inhabitant of Leeds. It is more complex than the recipe used by the present maker but similar to those pasties made in Yorkshire farmhouses until about 30 years ago, according to local historian Kate Mason. Mint pasties have been revived by at least one commercial baker after a gap of about 20 years in production.

TECHNIQUE:

The recipe given by Florence White requires shortcrust pastry (flour and fat in the ratio 2:1) to be rolled out thinly and cut into large rounds or squares. A thick filling of currants, raisins and candied peel layered with chopped fresh spearmint and brown sugar, topped with dabs of butter, grated nutmeg or other sweet spice is laid over one half of the pastry, the other is folded over the top, the edges dampened and pinched together. The pasty is baked at 220°C for about 30 minutes. Pasties produced commercially are simpler, based on currants only; white sugar and dried mint are substituted for the brown sugar and fresh mint.

REGION OF PRODUCTION:

North England, West Yorkshire.

Yorkshire Oatcake

DESCRIPTION:

An elongated oval, about 300mm long, 70mm wide, 2mm thick. Weight: approximately 45g. Colour: underside (closest to the bakstone when baked) is smooth gold-brown with a few unevenly scattered small holes and a paler line around the edge; the side which is uppermost during baking is rough, greyish and dusted with cream-coloured oatmeal. Flavour and texture: nutty, oaty, slightly sour; supple and soft when fresh, but crisp and hard once dry.

HISTORY:

The type of oatcake associated with Yorkshire and Lancashire during the past century has a long history and a highly evolved method attached to it. The climate of this region is cool and wet, and oats were the main cereal crop until the nineteenth century. The alternative name havercake is thought to be derived from Old Norse *hafre*, meaning oats.

Many travellers from the South of England commented on oatcakes and noted the distinct northern preference for them over wheat bread. Although consumption is now limited to parts of Yorkshire and Lancashire, with a second type finding favour in Staffordshire, the oatcake was once a staple of the entire region. Two distinct types existed: one made of dough, the other of batter. The stiffer dough was driven out thin by 'clapping' it with the hand on a special board. This is now extinct. The second was oatcake made with a pouring or runny batter. This might be spread by the complex 'throwing' method found in parts of Yorkshire and Lancashire, or could be poured on to the griddle as if a simple pancake – as found in the Midland counties of Stafford and Derby.

Yorkshire oatcakes are made from finely ground meal, mixed to a thin batter and leavened either by sourdough fermentation or yeast or, more recently, bicarbonate of soda. A complex method developed for shaking the batter until it became as thin as possible. It was riddled or shaken on a special wooden board scored with criss-cross lines, then slipped onto a hot bakstone (heated stone slab). This process is the origin of the variant name riddle cake or riddlebread. Later, an even more complex method evolved. Described by Frederic Montagu (1938), it began with riddling, but then the batter was slid on to a cloth and thence flicked on to the bakstone in a long, narrow and very thin trail. After 30 seconds or so on the bakstone, the cake was skimmed off with a spatula. Those not required straightaway were hung on a special rack to dry, after which they would keep indefinitely. Thin, light oatcakes were the most valued and a mechanical process, developed in the mid-nineteenth century, which required the batter to be scraped across the bakstone, was not considered to give good results. Several skilled oatcake bakers are recorded during the nineteenth century. Eventually, a machine for throwing oatcake batter was patented that met the specifications of oatcake aficionados. This was still in use in 1999.

Oatcakes were eaten fresh or dried with butter or treacle, or with cheese and beer in the fields. They were also dried and served soaked in gravy, or crumbled into broth, a mixture which was known as 'stew and hard'. Today, they are most likely to be eaten with cheese.

TECHNIQUE:

Fine oatmeal and water or buttermilk are mixed to a thin batter and left overnight to sour. The batter is placed in a wooden tub which is not cleaned between batches. More meal is stirred in next morning to give the right consistency. A riddling board is sprinkled with oatmeal and a ladleful of batter poured on top. The board is shaken with a rotary motion, and then the batter is slid on to a linen band, mounted on a trolley over the hot-plate. Using a handle, the trolley is moved rapidly across the hottest part of the hot-plate: the cloth band moves round, depositing the batter in a long trail over the plate. The oatcake remains over high heat for about 30 seconds and is then removed with a spatula to a cooler part of the plate to finish cooking. If soft oatcakes are required, they are removed at this point and allowed to cool. Hard oatcakes are dried off under the hot-plate.

REGION OF PRODUCTION:

North England, West Yorkshire, Lancashire.

Yorkshire Parkin

DESCRIPTION:

A ginger cake, customarily square, although now sometimes baked in round containers; 300mm square and 40–50mm deep is a typical size, usually sold in smaller portions. Weight: the size quoted would weigh about 2kg. Colour: dark chestnut, a shiny, sticky surface. Flavour and texture: very sweet, with distinct ginger flavour; sticky, clinging texture.

HISTORY:

Parkin goes under a variety of names or qualifications. Often, it is called after the county in which it is made: Yorkshire, Lancashire, and so on. Then there are the archaic names, for instance those found in South Yorkshire and Derbyshire of thar, thor or tharf cake. Moggy is the name for a wheat-flour parkin which is very sticky in texture.

Stead (1991) suggests the name thar cake is Middle English,

associated with the pre-Christmas Martinmas fast and, possibly, with pagan bonfire ceremonies which took place at the end of October (later christianized into All Souls). Parkin is still a customary food for the end of October and beginning of November, especially Bonfire Night (5 November). The name parkin or perkin (related to a diminutive of the Christian name Piers) is inexplicable but may denote affectionate disdain.

Parkin and thar cake were originally made on a griddle or bakestone. Suet, dripping, lard or butter were used depending on availability. The presence of spice would class it as a typical cake eaten on feast days and holidays, those moments in the year which justify extravagant ingredients. Some of the oatmeal was replaced by wheat flour in the 1800s, and the cake was further lightened by the addition of baking powder. The molasses was partly replaced by Golden Syrup when this product came on the market after 1880. Parkin is produced by al-most every craft baker in the North Country.

TECHNIQUE:

Ingredients are equal quantities of oatmeal and wheat flour. Golden Syrup, sugar, and butter are used – each about a third the amount of the total flour. Molasses or black treacle may be substituted for part of the syrup. Additions are ginger, to flavour; a little baking powder to leaven; and milk to mix. Some people add an egg. The syrup or treacle, sugar and butter are heated gently together and stirred; in a separate container, the dry ingredients are blended. The mixtures are amalgamated; milk and egg (if required) are mixed for a soft, runny dough; this is poured into a well-lined tin. It is baked at 180°C for 60–90 minutes. The cooled parkin is wrapped in paper or foil and left for a few days before eating.

REGION OF PRODUCTION:

NORTH ENGLAND, YORKSHIRE AND LANCASHIRE.

Yorkshire Teacake

DESCRIPTION:

A circular bun about 30mm deep, 100–110mm across, sometimes larger. Weight: about 75g for the size given. Colour and texture: golden crust, speckled with fruit, fading to white at the base, paler brown underneath; crumb soft but not open, off-white, with well-distributed currants. Flavour: fresh bread smell, with fruity sweetness from currants; candied peel is sometimes added, although it is uncommon; sweet mixed spice (cinnamon, cloves, nutmeg) is the typical aroma.

HISTORY:

The compound word tea-cake is listed from the 1830s in the *OED*. Who is to say what precisely was being denoted? Was it that the drink needed a solid companion? Or was it that a new meal, tea, was a moment in the day celebrated by the production of sweet breads?

Yorkshire teacakes were at first just Yorkshire cakes. That is the name given them in 1817, in the earliest recipe so far located (David, 1977). It is a lightly enriched dough with milk, eggs and a little butter, similar to that still used, but with no fruit. They had become teacakes by the time of Cassell (1896) who wrote, 'a hospitable Yorkshire housewife would consider her tea-table was barely spread if it were not liberally supplied with these delicious cakes, constant relays of which should be served steaming hot.' If the transformation of cakes into teacakes is a mark of one small social revolution, the firm association of Yorkshire with these buns must also be indication of some reality of social geography. We are reduced to speculating that the county was a place with a reputation for good baking and a tradition of high tea, a large early-evening meal involving many baked items.

That regional affiliation has long vanished, although the cakes are still valued in Yorkshire. Industrial production has meant their spread throughout the country.

TECHNIQUE:

Teacakes are made with an enriched bread dough. Kirkland (1907) wrote that they were on the borderline between bread and buns. By this he meant that the fermentation was usually a two-stage affair – a yeast, flour and water sponge followed by mixing in the fat, fruit, sugar and eggs (if used) – and that they were only lightly enriched. The ratio of fat to flour is about 1:3. The fat is either lard or butter. They are baked at 240–250°C for 15–20 minutes.

REGION OF PRODUCTION:

North England.

Coltsfoot Rock

DESCRIPTION:

Hexagonal sticks 10cm long, 1cm diameter. Weight: 10g. Colour: light brown. Flavour: sweet, herbal, aniseed. Composition: sugar, liquorice, gelatine, paregoric, capsicum, oil of aniseed, coltsfoot extract (.0012 per cent).

HISTORY:

Coltsfoot, *Tussilargo farfara*, was long used as a remedy for chest infections. Culpeper's *Herbal* gives coughwort as an alternative name. It was also used to bolster meagre supplies of tobacco, much as boys would once smoke old man's beard. When a medicine, it was used as juice or made into syrup. From an early date, it was probably used for flavouring boiled sugar or sugar paste, but Mayhew's (1851) description of a street-vendor with coltsfoot sticks amongst his wares is the first known reference. A recipe in Skuse's *Confectioner's Handbook* (*c.* 1892) shows them to have been a paste of gum tragacanth, liquorice, aniseed, lemon essence and sugar extruded as sticks. The modern version appears essentially unchanged. It now has a strong regional identity, particularly with West Yorkshire and Lancashire. Until the 1950s, several companies produced it, now but one manufacturer survives, Stockley Sweets Ltd of Oswaldtwistle, Accrington, Lancashire.

TECHNIQUE:

The rock is made from sugar paste by a simple mixing of sugar, gums, water and coltsfoot essence to the correct consistency; this is extruded in sticks, allowed to dry for 2 days and packaged.

REGION OF PRODUCTION:

North England, West Yorkshire, Lancashire.

Lily Of The Valley Creams

DESCRIPTION:

Chocolates filled with firm, white-sugar fondant, 25mm diameter, 20mm deep. Weight: 12g. Composition: chocolate, sugar, flavouring. Other flower flavourings used for fondant-filled chocolates in England are rose and violet. Fruit, mint and coffee flavours are more common.

HISTORY:

England has a long tradition of using flowers to flavour sugar syrups. It can be seen in some of the earliest confectionery texts, such as Sir Hugh Plat's *Delightes for Ladies*, in which roses, violets, borage, cowslips, gillyflowers (carnation pinks), marigolds and rosemary are mentioned. This continued into the eighteenth century when they were made into little 'cakes' of sugar. It is not clear if these were high-boiled, clear drops or similar to the modern grained-sugar Kendal mint cake. Mary Eales (1733) called one of her flower-flavoured recipes 'honeycomb cakes'. This sort of sweet was probably made wherever suitable flowers grew, but the skill and expense involved limited production to professional confectioners and the still-rooms of the wealthy. Their audience was only enlarged once confectioners adopted industrial techniques. Thereafter, grained-sugar fondant became a popular filling for chocolates, often with floral perfumes. Old-fashioned rose and violet flavours are still used by some companies.

One is Bonnet's of Scarborough, founded by a Swiss immigrant in 1880. It has always used flower essences in a range of confectionery much coveted as souvenir of this elegant resort. The firm was almost certainly responsible for the wallflower creams remembered from his youth by Compton Mackenzie (1954). The range has become ever more limited as the necessary essences are difficult to obtain, but it still makes one perfumed with lily of the valley.

TECHNIQUE:

Few, if any, chocolatiers make their own fondant any longer. Instead it is bought in blocks and mixed with ingredients such as glycerine and flavouring essences. Some, like Bonnet's, use starch-moulding to produce the fondant centres: the fondant is melted and poured into impressions made in trays of fine starch and then allowed to set. Once the pieces are firm enough to handle, they are carefully removed, rid of excess starch, then coated with chocolate, either by hand-dipping (in a few companies) or enrobing. The chocolates are decorated, left to set, then displayed or packed for distribution.

REGION OF PRODUCTION:

North England, Yorkshire.

Pontefract Cakes

DESCRIPTION:

Tablets of liquorice, 30mm diameter, 4mm thick, a design stamped on one face. Weight: 4–6g. Colour: shiny black. Flavour: sweet liquorice and aniseed; tough, chewy texture.

HISTORY:

The town of Pontefract in south Yorkshire was first noted for liquorice cultivation in the mid-1600s, although the plant had probably grown there for longer. The juice from its roots was used to treat colds and chest complaints. Though there is no written evidence, it is likely that from a very early date the juice was also boiled into a compound that could be chewed or sucked. A seal dated 1614 found in the town bears a design similar to that used on the face of modern Pontefract cakes. (The owl that forms part of the crest belongs to the heraldic device of the Savile family, local landowners.)

The first cakes that were recognizable as those of today are dated to 1760, when a local apothecary, George Dunhill, is said to have added sugar to the recipe. Thereafter, the industry prospered, first using locally-produced liquorice, later relying on imported block juice. In 1893, 11 manufacturers were listed, all of whom made Pontefract cakes.

An industry based on imported juice still flourishes even though cultivation of the plant has ceased. Two manufacturers of Pontefract cakes and other confectionery remain.

TECHNIQUE:

The ingredients are listed as treacle, wheat flour, sugar, water, caramel, liquorice extract, salt, invertase, artificial flavours. The exact process is a trade secret. A batch method for producing liquorice is as follows. Water and flour are blended and heated to boiling. Water, sugar and block juice are mixed separately, then treacle and glucose syrup added and brought to the boil. The mixtures are amalgamated, and cooked. Caramel, aniseed, gelatine, colours and flavours are added and mixed through. The mixture is extruded to give the desired shape. After moulding, liquorice is stoved at 40–50°C for 12–24 hours. It is conditioned for 1 day at 20°C and 50 per cent relative humidity. It may then be packed for sale.

REGION OF PRODUCTION:

North England, Pontefract (South Yorkshire).

Treacle Toffee

DESCRIPTION:

A hard, crunchy confection sold from open trays 400mm wide, 200mm long, 10mm deep. Colour: chestnut to deep brown. Flavour and texture: sweet with buttery overtones, slight bitter note if black treacle or molasses is used; hard, slightly tough. Composition: sugar, Golden Syrup or treacle, butter.

HISTORY:

The origin of the word toffee is obscure. It has been used since at least the early 1800s. Sometimes spelt taffy, it may be derived from tough or toughy, describing the texture of toffee made to early recipes (*OED*). These often involved pulling the sugar, which made it harder. There is a possible link with the word tafia, a rum-like drink made from molasses. The persistent use of molasses, black treacle and, later, Golden Syrup in toffee supports this idea. Toffee is also used by sugar-boilers as a general term to indicate high-boiled sugar, and some early toffee recipes (such as that for Everton toffee, once very famous) are closer to the modern concept of butterscotch.

Nor are the beginnings of toffee well documented. Only the recipe for Everton toffee appears to have been thought worth recording. But, during the 1800s, toffee of many types was obviously known and loved, and 'toffee-pulls' were social gatherings for young people. Presumably the variants were so well known to cooks and back-street confectioners that no-one thought any more of them. The first published recipe for treacle toffee so far discovered is from the first decades of the twentieth century. By this time, one of the best known names in toffee, John Mackintosh, had established his factory in Halifax, West Yorkshire, where he produced treacle toffee and the newly fashionable soft American caramels. Many other companies, large and small, produced toffee in these same years, but among those who survive today, the old treacle toffee accounts for a fraction of their output; softer, more chewy toffees are now favoured. In the North country this hard treacle toffee was often called Bonfire toffee or Plot toffee in recognition of the fact that it was made as part of the celebrations surrounding the night of 5 November, Bonfire Night.

TECHNIQUE:

An old recipe used by toffee-boilers calls for black treacle, soft light brown sugar and butter in the proportions 2:2:1; these are brought to the boil, with the addition of a little water and tartaric acid or vinegar, and cooked to 125°C. The mixture is poured into buttered tins and cooled. In the past, it was then then distributed to shops and newsagents where a special little hammer is used to break the hard toffee into irregular pieces, weighed out as the customer requires. Less traditionally, perhaps more hygienically, it is now broken and pre-packed in Cellophane.

The sugar – white, pale or dark brown, fine or coarse – and the treacle – golden, black or molasses – are variable. Some recipes call for milk or, in commerce, condensed milk; the quantity of butter may be reduced accordingly. Glucose is now usually added, rather than relying on the action of tartaric acid or vinegar to achieve the correct texture. Modern recipes show a tendency to a lower proportion of black treacle and more brown sugar or Golden Syrup. Modern versions of toffee are rarely pulled.

REGION OF PRODUCTION:

North England.

Bitter Beer (Tadcaster): Samuel Smith's Old Brewery Strong Pale Ale

DESCRIPTION:

This beer is dark copper in colour, sweetish, hoppy and relatively full-bodied. It is 5 per cent alcohol by volume. The company also produces a stronger beer called Museum Ale. These are brewed by the 'Yorkshire squares' method, used by others in the area, notably the Black Sheep (Masham, using stone squares), and Tetley's (Leeds, using stainless steel). Tadcaster has 3 breweries but the others (Bass Charrington and John Smith's) do not use the method. Bitters from Tadcaster are sometimes called pale ales.

HISTORY:

Tadcaster's association with good brewing goes back to the Middle Ages, due in part to the water, drawn from wells which penetrate limestone strata. Samuel Smith's brewery was founded in 1758. In the 1840s, 2 brothers divided the business between them, one branch continuing at Samuel Smith's, the other as John Smith's, now subsumed into a larger group. The Yorkshire squares system is known in other towns in the area and its use has been recorded to the south, on the border with Nottingham. Its origin is unknown. Jackson (1993) notes a suggestion that its development was linked with a scientific paper on the absorption of gases in liquids, published in the late eighteenth century by a Leeds chemist. It is associated with strains of yeast which lend distinctive characteristics to beers produced by the method.

TECHNIQUE:

Brewing commences with a mash of malt and liquor drawn from the brewery's own wells; the wort is strained off into a brew kettle and boiled with Goldings and Fuggles hops for 60–90 minutes; the wort is strained and cooled and the yeast strain favoured by Smith's added. Fermentation begins in the lower half of large, covered, slate-lined square tanks. As the yeast begins to work, the wort rises through an opening in the top of the tank and overflows into a second tank above; then the beer settles and sinks back, leaving a yeast residue behind. This cycle is repeated several times in the 4–5 days it takes for fermentation to complete. About halfway through, the beer is 'roused' by pumping it from the lower to the upper tank through a pipe, encouraging the yeast to work more. When the beer rises for the final time, it is skimmed and led into settling tanks. It is racked into wooden casks, allowed to stand for 3–4 days and primed and fined. If it is bottled, it is first filtered and pasteurized.

REGION OF PRODUCTION:

NORTH ENGLAND, TADCASTER (YORKSHIRE).

Black Beer

DESCRIPTION:

BLACK BEER IS VERY DARK BROWN; ITS FLAVOUR IS SWEET-BITTER WITH MALTY, MOLASSES OVERTONES. IT IS 8.5 PER CENT ALCOHOL BY VOLUME.

HISTORY:

The drink originated as a prophylactic against scurvy. It was carried as part of ships' stores and was drunk mixed with rum. Jackson (1993) notes possible relationships with spruce beer, which included the tips of spruce branches in the mash and must have had a distinctly resinous flavour. This was known in the Baltic states and is also drunk on the eastern seaboard of Canada. Beers like this, used primarily as mixers and dietary supplements, were extensively made in the north of England. There were about 6 companies involved at the end of the nineteenth century, but by the 1970s only one survived. The beer is still made in Yorkshire, where various folk traditions have grown up around it: one often met is that a pregnant woman who drinks it will give birth to twins. It is not clear if it is the same black beer that was served in the temperance bars of neighbouring Lancashire up to the 1920s.

The remaining company which makes black beer is owned by a larger group producing ciders, perries and other English drinks. Unlike other alcoholic drinks, black beer, because it is used as a mixer and has a high original gravity in relation to alcoholic content, is exempt from duty under UK and EU laws. It may be mixed with milk, lemonade or rum (in which case it is known as 'rum and black'); it also added to fruit cakes and Christmas puddings.

TECHNIQUE:

For black beer, the malt is mashed and the wort concentrated; this step was once carried out by the manufacturer, but the original equipment proved too costly and it is now prepared by the Association of British Maltsters. This is blended with barley syrup and raw cane sugar and fermented with a specialized yeast. It is allowed to settle before pasteurization and bottling.

REGION OF PRODUCTION:

NORTH ENGLAND, LEEDS (YORKSHIRE).

Dandelion And Burdock

DESCRIPTION:

AVAILABLE AS A CORDIAL OR READY-DILUTED WITH SODA WATER. IT IS DARK COPPER-BROWN IN COLOUR AND SLIGHTLY ANISEED, MILDLY BITTER IN FLAVOUR.

HISTORY:

Dandelion, *Taraxacum officinale*, and burdock, *Arctium Lappa*, were both recognized for their medicinal qualities in Britain from early times, in particular as blood purifiers, useful in early spring. Burdock was also used to flavour ale before hops became the most common addition (Dunkling, 1992). During the latter half of the nineteenth century, herbal drinks were promoted as an alternative to beer and spirits. Apart from dandelion and burdock, perhaps sarsaparilla is the best known. The companies which now manufacture this drink have their origins in the temperance movement. One, Ben Shaw's of Huddersfield, West Yorkshire, began in 1871, when Ben Shaw set up in partnership with his brother, as Shaw Brothers, Manufacturers of Non-alcoholic Beverages. The company manufactured various drinks including Horehound Beer, Dandelion Stout and Botanic Porter. Some of the early 'non-alcoholic' drinks were brewed. The company's first registered trademark was a dandelion plant. Another much smaller company still making the drink is Herbal Health, based in Lancashire; their premises include the last-known temperance bar in Britain. There are 3 known producers.

TECHNIQUE:

A mixture of herbal extracts, flavourings and sugar syrup is used; either sold as a cordial or diluted with carbonated water and bottled.

REGION OF PRODUCTION:

NORTH ENGLAND, WEST YORKSHIRE AND EAST LANCASHIRE.

Oatmeal Stout

DESCRIPTION:

Almost black with deep red lights and a beige head. It has a fruity aroma, rounded nutty flavour and a smooth, silky, almost oily texture. It is 5 per cent alcohol by volume.

HISTORY:

Oats were malted for beer in parts of northern and western Britain in the late medieval period. However, it is a difficult grain for brewers to work with as it gelatinizes at mashing temperatures. Mostly, it is used mixed in small proportions with other grains. Oatmeal stout as known today owes much to the fashion for brewing 'nutritious' beers current during the late nineteenth and early twentieth centuries. Oatmeal stouts have been produced in small quantities ever since. Eldridge Pope (Dorset) brewed one until 1975, and Samuel Smith's revived the style in 1980. Several breweries now produce them. Such dark, heavy beers are generally more favoured as winter drinks.

TECHNIQUE:

In Britain, oats are typically northern. Production of oatmeal stout is like that of other British beers save that a proportion of oats is added to the brewing grain; in some cases these are rolled oats. Samuel Smith's uses pale ale, crystal and roasted barley malts to make its oatmeal stout, and the beer is fermented for about 12 hours longer than ordinary bitter beers.

REGION OF PRODUCTION:

North England, Yorkshire.

Old Peculier

DESCRIPTION:

Old Peculier is dark brown; its flavour is heavy, rich and sweet. This sort of beer has a high original gravity because it contains much sugar; alcohol content is variable, usually 5.5–8.5 per cent.

HISTORY:

The concept of old ale as a beer evoking nostalgia for the good things of the past dates back at least a century in Britain and is primarily an English style (Jackson, 1993). The brews are generally sweetish and rich, supposedly recalling dark beers from the 1700s. It is, however, a field in which brewers are very idiosyncratic, and there are no hard rules. Wilson (1983) notes that very strong ales were being brewed by the sixteenth century, and that in the seventeenth century, Yorkshire ale was drunk stale old and strong. The best was said to come from Northallerton. There is a seventeenth-century poem in praise of the ales of Northallerton and Thirsk. These towns are near Masham, where Old Peculier originated. The brewery, T. & R. Theakston, was founded in 1827. It is claimed that Old Peculier has been made from the early days and has been known under this name since the 1890s. It derives from the town having its own peculiar, or separate ecclesiastical jurisdiction. The seal is used as a trademark by the brewery.

During the 1980s, Theakston's was bought by Scottish & Newcastle Breweries and now only that part of the production of the beer intended for the North Yorkshire market is brewed in Masham. Many other brewers make strong, dark, sweetish beers – known as old, winter or strong ales, but often given fanciful names. They are more popular in cold weather and some only brew in mid-winter.

TECHNIQUE:

Brewing begins with a mash of crushed pale ale and crystal malts and torrefied wheat mixed with liquor (water heated to 70°C), brewer's caramel and 3 types of sugar. The wort is strained into a brew kettle and boiled with English hops; Fuggles (for aroma) are added towards the end of boiling; then the wort is strained, cooled and Theakston's yeast added. Fermentation is in vessels of the Yorkshire squares type for 4–5 days after which the beer is either fined and dry-hopped with more Fuggles and put into casks, or brewery-conditioned in large tanks before filtering, fining, pasteurizing and bottling.

REGION OF PRODUCTION:

North England, Masham (North Yorkshire).

Raspberry Vinegar

DESCRIPTION:

Raspberry vinegar is a deep, clear red, with a sweet-acid flavour and distinct raspberry taste.

HISTORY:

Recipes for flavoured vinegars were common, often using herbs but also fruit. Those for raspberry usually required wine or cider vinegar to be flavoured with the fruit and sweetened with sugar. It was recommended, diluted, as a soothing drink for sore throats and fevers, and in hot weather. Recipes for a version based on malt vinegar appear in local collections in the north of England in the late nineteenth and early twentieth centuries. It is not clear when malt was substituted for wine vinegar. As the former was cheap and commonly available, it is possible that it had always been used by poorer people. *Law's Grocer's Manual* (*c.* 1895) mentions it could easily be made at home with raspberries and ordinary (malt) vinegar, and gives the addresses of 2 London manufacturers.

As drinks, flavoured vinegars went out of fashion before 1939–45. Raspberry vinegar lingered in the north and east of England because of a strong tradition of using it as a condiment for Yorkshire pudding.

During the 1970s and 1980s, flavoured vinegars were rediscovered by cooks and have again become popular.

TECHNIQUE:

For a raspberry vinegar of the type used as a condiment for Yorkshire pudding, the proportions are 500g fresh fruit: 700ml malt vinegar: 500g sugar. The fruit is washed and soaked in the vinegar in a cool place for 4 days. The liquid is strained off, then sugar dissolved in it and boiled for 15 minutes. It is cooled, strained and bottled.

Other flavourings were once common: red currants, blackberries, gooseberries, roses and elderflowers were all used to make drinks and condiments; herbs, spices, horseradish, shallots or garlic and chillies were steeped in vinegar for pickling or as a store sauce to be added to meat. Many are enjoying a revival. Some manufacturers import wine vinegar, but many use cider or spirit (distilled malt) vinegar, plus fruit, flowers and herbs available in their locality.

REGION OF PRODUCTION:

NORTH ENGLAND.

Yorkshire Relish

DESCRIPTION:

EACH VARIETY OF YORKSHIRE RELISH HAS ITS OWN APPEARANCE: 'THIN' IS DARK BROWN; 'SPICY' AND 'FRUITY' ARE THICKER AND REDDISH-BROWN. THE FLAVOUR IS FRUITY (DATES, TAMARIND) AND ACIDIC.

HISTORY:

This is one of a group of patent sauces manufactured under trademarks to secret recipes in Britain for over a hundred years. Yorkshire Relish was registered in 1877.

The use of relish in the sense of a sharp substance which provided a contrast, making something else taste sweeter, is old. It was well enough known for an author to use it in the early 1600s as a metaphor when writing about life not being unmingled happiness, but 'having some sour sauce to relish it'. Though the word had wider currency – to do with pleasure and strong flavours in eating and drinking generally – the mention of 'sour sauce' is interesting. Modern Yorkshire Relish could still be described thus.

The sauce known today originated in 1837, when Robert Goodall, a Leeds chemist, started to bottle the thin type, which was made by his wife. It is mentioned in the *Trademarks Journal* in 1877, when the firm had expanded to become Goodall, Backhouse & Co. There was a vigorous advertising campaign in the 1880s. The production of Thick Yorkshire Relish commenced in 1932. Like other English brown sauces it is based on tamarinds and secret spice mixtures. They were imitations of Indian sauces and chutneys. The methods and spices were Indian, buttressed by vinegar and home-grown fruit and vegetables. Eliza Acton's 'Bengal Receipt' for 'Chatney sauce', based on unripe plums or crab apples, spices, sugar and vinegar, would probably give a result quite similar to modern brown sauces.

In 1959 Hammond's, another sauce company based in Yorkshire, already making the relishes under licence, acquired Goodall's. Although there have been 3 subsequent mergers, the name Yorkshire Relish survives and it is still produced in the Leeds area.

TECHNIQUE:

The ingredients of Thick Yorkshire Relish are tomatoes, date purée, sugar, apple purée, malt vinegar, flour, soy sauce concentrate, salt, molasses, spirit vinegar, acetic acid, onions, spices, tamarind concentrate, colour (caramel), garlic, stabilizer (Karaya gum), hydrolyzed vegetable protein, flavouring.

The method is a trade secret but is essentially a simple process of mixing and cooking in open pans. The sauce can be used as soon as it is made but benefits from a short maturation.

REGION OF PRODUCTION:

WEST YORKSHIRE.

North East England

Pease Pudding

DESCRIPTION:

Pease pudding is a solid purée, sold by weight. Colour: pale orange-yellow. Flavour: distinct, earthy, pulse flavour; often salty.

HISTORY:

Every British child used to learn the rhyme, 'Pease pudding hot, pease pudding cold, pease pudding in the pot, nine days old,' which asserted the pulse's ubiquity, longevity, as well as monotony, when diet was limited by primitive transport and preservation methods.

Dishes made from dried peas were associated with Lent and fasting, 'Pease pudding developed from the old pottages of dried peas which were a national dish in England during the sixteenth and seventeenth centuries, known in French recipe books as "pottage in the English style"' (Wilson, 1973). Popularity declined during the eighteenth century and the pudding gradually became regionalized to North-East England. Because it is an accompaniment for salted pork, as in pease pudding and boiled bacon – there are medieval instructions for the identical combination (Hieatt, 1986) – it is made and sold by pork butchers.

Mushy peas, sold throughout Britain in fish-and-chips shops or pie shops, are also a purée based on dried peas.

TECHNIQUE:

Split yellow peas are soaked and cooked in water until they disintegrate to a purée. They are seasoned to taste, usually just with salt, poured into a bowl and left to cool. Alternatively, salty stock from cooking bacon can be used to cook the peas. The housewife seasons and enriches it with butter and egg as desired, and reheats the mixture.

REGION OF PRODUCTION:

NORTH EAST ENGLAND.

Cotherstone Cheese

DESCRIPTION:

PRESSED, PASTEURIZED COW'S MILK CHEESE. DIMENSIONS VARY ACCORDING TO WEIGHT; ONE WEIGHING 1KG IS APPROXIMATELY 12CM DIAMETER AND 8CM HIGH. WEIGHT: MADE IN SIZES OF ABOUT 500G–3KG. FORM: A SMALL MILLSTONE. COLOUR: PALE CREAMY YELLOW WITH A FEW SMALL, IRREGULAR HOLES. WHEN MATURED IN A HUMID ATMOSPHERE IT DEVELOPS A PINKY-GOLD COLOUR ON THE RIND. FLAVOUR AND TEXTURE: MILD, ACID FLAVOUR, BUTTERY LACTIC AFTERTASTE; A SMOOTH CREAMY TEXTURE.

HISTORY:

Cotherstone takes its name from a village in Teesdale, on the Durham–Yorkshire border. It was mentioned as early as 1911, when it was noted in the *Encyclopaedia Britannica* (Rance, 1982). It shares the same general history as the Swaledale, Wensleydale and Coverdale made just to the south, inheriting a common tradition of cheese-making from medieval monasteries. However, Cotherstone thinks itself proudly individual. Manufacture suffered, as did all other British cheeses, from centralization of cheese-making during 1939–45 and its after-effects. One of these was a deep conviction held by many that farm-made cheese was not allowed by the Milk Marketing Board, the body set up to control the fresh milk supply. Consequently, on-farm cheese-making in the area survived on a very small scale. In 1956, Simon recorded it as 'a double-cream cheese which repaid keeping and watching: it was similar to Stilton both as to shape and size. It was farm-made, very good, but never made in large quantities.' In the past, some of these cheeses are reported to have blued naturally, although the present maker does not achieve this. This type of mild cheese is often eaten with fruit cake and apple pie in Yorkshire.

TECHNIQUE:

Pasteurized milk from Friesian cattle grazed in Teesdale is used. The maker remarks that its distinctive nature is probably derived from the local flora. A basic recipe commences by leaving the evening milk to set and, in the morning, skimming the cream, heating it, and returning it to the milk together with the morning's milk. The milk is brought to 21°C and starter added; the temperature raised to 27°C, and rennet added once the correct acidity is reached. It is stirred until setting begins. It is then left for an hour. The curd is cubed gently and the temperature raised gradually to 30°C whilst stirring gently; then it is allowed to settle until the acidity is correct. The whey is drained. The curd is cut into large cubes, milled and salted (12g salt to 1kg curd), then lightly packed into lined moulds and pressed for about 12 hours. After removing the binding, the cheeses are ripened for 2–3 weeks before selling, but can be matured successfully for up to 2 months, given suitable temperature and humidity.

Cotherstone was once made from spring until the first frost but is now available all year.

REGION OF PRODUCTION:

North East England.

Kipper (Craster)

DESCRIPTION:

A whole herring split from mouth to tail, with gills and internal organs removed but backbone intact, cold smoked. Kippers from this area are generally small, 22–23cm from head to tail, weighing 140–150g each. Colour: the skin is grey-brown, dark on the back, fading gradually to silver on the belly; the flesh is pale gold-brown. Flavour: a good balance of salt and smoke, with neither predominating; oily flesh.

HISTORY:

Some discussion of the meaning of the word kipper is to be found in the entry relating to smoked salmon of Scotland (p. 369). The *Oxford English Dictionary* itself is not sure about the transition from a word describing a spent salmon to a definition of a type of cure. All that can be said is that a fish cure which consisted of brining followed by drying and smoking was known as kippering; that it was applied to both salmon and herring treated this way; and that it has links with the north-eastern coast around the Scottish Borders and with Scotland itself.

The origin of the kipper in a modern sense, referring exclusively to cured smoked herring, is usually attributed to John Woodger who worked at Seahouses on the Northumbrian coast in the 1840s. The 'Newcastle Kipper', as it was first called, was deliberately invented after several years of experiment, and was first sent to London in 1846, based on the 'kippered salmon' of the area; 'Woodger transferred the epithet to the herring smoked overnight after splitting down the back, removing the guts and gills, and lightly salting, originally in solid salt' (Cutting, 1955). According to Alan Robson, whose family have made kippers in Craster for at least 3 generations, the smokehouse currently used was built in 1856.

The production of kippers in spring and summer meant that they did not compete with the cured herring produced in Yarmouth, which came from the autumn catch. The East-coast herring fishery was a migratory affair, progressing southwards as the year advanced. The work at sea was supported on land by a mobile labour force, principally Scottish and female, who followed the herring down the coast gutting, filleting and processing. Craster's kipper season fitted nicely into this seashore transhumance.

TECHNIQUE:

Herrings landed from May to late August are used for kippers. These are now difficult to obtain as the decline in herring stocks, the introduction of freezing at sea, and patterns in marketing fish have affected ports in the North-East. It is quite possible that fish caught in the area may now be taken north and landed at Fraserburgh on the Scottish coast, where the catch is certain to find a good market.

Kippers from the North-East are small, selected with size and oil content (12–20 per cent) in mind. On arrival at the smokehouse, the fish are split and gutted mechanically. They are brined for about 20 minutes. The fish are stretched open on tenterhooks or wooden pegs and hung in rows on frames; these are suspended in the smokehouses. Fires of oak sawdust are burnt for 12–16 hours, depending on size and weather. A properly smoked kipper will keep for about a week.

REGION OF PRODUCTION:

North East England, Craster (Northumbria).

COMPARE WITH:

Kipper (Manx), Isle of Man (p. 1); Kipper (Whitby) below.

Kipper (Whitby)

DESCRIPTION:

A whole cold-smoked herring, split from mouth to tail, with gills and internal organs removed, but backbone left intact; those from Whitby are split through the back rather than the belly, which is the normal practice. Examples of kippers recently obtained from Whitby are large, about 27–30cm from head to tail, weighing about 270–300g. Colour: Whitby kippers are relatively dark gold brown, with dark skin on the backs and silvery below; the skin of a Norfolk kipper is grey-silver on the back, silver-white on the belly, with pale, pink-brown flesh. Flavour: Whitby kippers have a powerful smoke flavour.

HISTORY:

After the kipper cure for herrings was invented in the 1840s on the Northumbrian coast, it spread rapidly southwards. John Woodger, the inventor, set up a kipper processing works in Yarmouth, capitalizing on the locally landed fish and the skilled labour provided by the migrant

Scottish 'herring lassies' who followed the shoals south through the summer to work in the towns where herrings were landed at different times of the season. The words of the Gaelic poet Iain Crichton Smith, born on the Isle of Lewis, in *To My Mother* are apposite: 'You were gutting herring in distant Yarmouth and the salt sun in the morning rising out of the sea, the blood on the edge of your knife, and that salt so coarse that it stopped you from speaking and made your lips bitter …'

The same process was also adopted in Whitby, where kippers have also been made for over a hundred years; one maker, Fortune's, is in the fourth generation. The industry, as everywhere else, has been affected by the decline in herring catches since the 1950s.

TECHNIQUE:

No herring have been landed in Whitby since the 1970s. By the time the herring have travelled further south, and arrived off the East Anglian coast, they are often too low in oil content to make successful kippers. Therefore, kipper curers in both locations buy fish from wherever a suitable size and oil content can be obtained, usually from Icelandic or Norwegian waters. Cures vary slightly between makers. Fortune's, in Whitby, salt the fish for about 40 minutes and smoke them for 16–30 hours, depending on the weather. The kippers are always sold in pairs (presented with the split sides together). The selection of wood for smoking herrings is, to some extent, down to the personal preference of the maker, but most favour oak.

REGION OF PRODUCTION:

NORTH EAST ENGLAND, WHITBY (NORTH YORKSHIRE); EAST ANGLIA, GREAT YARMOUTH, (NORFOLK).

COMPARE WITH:

Kipper (Craster), above.

Pig's Trotters

DESCRIPTION:

Pigs' feet, cleaned and sometimes brined, displayed ready-cooked on trays. Trotters can be seen for sale in old-fashioned butcher's shops.

HISTORY:

Animal feet were once more used in the British kitchen than they are today. They were valued both as a source of gelatine and as meat in their own right. They were available to any house-holder who killed a beast, or could be cheaply purchased from butchers. Since at least the sixteenth century, the word for animal feet when used as food has been trotters; however, some regions still refer to pig's trotters as pig's feet. They were not considered elegant, and are now mostly a food of the urban poor or of the gormandizing, probably francophile, middle classes. Like many kinds of offal in Britain, they now have a strong association with the food habits of South Lancashire. There has always been a good market for pre-prepared food in this area, as many women still worked after marriage, and both pig's feet and sheep's feet were popular here until quite recently. Sheep's feet have almost disappeared from the menu, due to changing tastes and the prolonged handiwork required to prepare them for the market, but pig's feet are still easily available.

TECHNIQUE:

Pigs' trotters are cleaned thoroughly, cooked in brine and cooled before being sold.

REGION OF PRODUCTION:

Pigs' feet are available nationally; sheep's feet are rarely seen for sale outside Lancashire.

The brown crab fishery on South Wight is managed by just a few longshoremen from families who, according to island interpretation, make a living from the beach. This can mean anything from keeping the beach clean and putting out deck chairs to helping a sailor with a heavy dinghy. Among the families, who go back up to 400 years, are the Wheelers and the Blakes. The Blakes sell their fish in Ventnor and the Wheelers are a few minutes' walk away on Steephill Cove. Recently, the ministry responsible for fisheries (DEFRA) contributed to the building of a small 'haven' harbour in Ventnor, a safe place for boats to come in and out in all weather. Previously, the fishermen could only fish when the weather was good enough to drag returning boats onto the beach, so this commonsense policy has done much to preserve a way of life. The longshoremen families in South Wight manage their fishery carefully, but this is not the only element that will ensure a future for the Isle of Wight crab: Cheryl Blake's cheerful shop on Ventnor's esplanade sells the freshest picked crab to nibble on the beach and the Wheelers run an excellent restaurant – the Boathouse – at Steephill Cove. Crab pasties, steaming hot from the oven of a neighbouring fisherman's cottage, are offered for sale to grateful walkers.

Rose Prince

AUTHOR OF *THE NEW ENGLISH KITCHEN*

Isle of Wight Crab Pasties

Makes 5

1 slice of wholemeal bread
240g (8oz) crabmeat, brown and white
120g (4oz) leeks, chopped
2 tsp lemon juice
walnut-sized piece of butter, melted
¼ teaspoon salt
a pinch of turmeric
480g (1lb) puff pastry
a little milk
freshly ground black pepper

Preheat the oven to 200°C/400°F/Gas Mark 6. Chop the bread in a food processor, transfer to a bowl and stir in the crabmeat, leeks, lemon juice, melted butter, salt, turmeric and some pepper. Roll out the puff pastry thinly and cut out five circles about 15cm (6 inches) each in diameter. Place a heap of the crab mixture in the centre of each one. Brush the edges with milk and then fold over and pinch them together to form a pasty. Brush the tops of the pasties with milk, place them on a baking tray and bake for about thirty minutes, until golden. Serve straight from the oven.

Stotty Cake

DESCRIPTION:

An irregular, thick disc, sometimes with a small hole roughly in the centre; 200mm diameter, 30mm deep. Weight: about 270g. Colour and texture: white around the edges, and around the hole in the middle; brown in irregular patches over the rest of the surface; dusted with flour; crusty texture.

HISTORY:

The origin of the name stottie, or stotty, is unknown and little notice seems to have been taken of it until well into the twentieth century. The word stot in North-Eastern dialect has several meanings, one of which is to bounce or rebound. Lillian Patterson, of Gregg's Bakers in Newcastle-upon-Tyne, says this name is given to the cakes because the dough was stotted or thrown on to the floor of the oven. The Yorkshire name for the same item, oven-bottom cake, simply reflects the baking method. Another name, scuffler, is current in Yorkshire, perhaps referring to the process of cleaning the oven bottom of ash before baking commences – the tool used was a scuffle. Brears (1987) and Spicer (1948) show the bread was made before the Second World War. Stotties were made from ordinary bread dough. They may be likened to Italian or French hearth-breads that were made from the main batch of dough and baked as a preliminary before the oven was fully charged. Stotties were also an economical way with leftovers from the main batch of dough: knead them all together and roll them out. They are popular for making sandwiches, cut or pulled apart horizontally and filled with ham or bacon. Instead of spreading with butter before filling the bread, people in the North-East some-times prefer pease pudding.

TECHNIQUE:

After bulk fermentation, the dough is knocked back and divided into pieces which are patted into large discs. These are pricked, or a hole is made in the centre, and then proved. They are baked on the oven floor at about 200°C for 15 minutes. They are then turned and allowed to bake another 15 minutes at a slightly reduced temperature.

REGION OF PRODUCTION:

North East England, Yorkshire, Durham, southern Northumberland.

Berwick Cockles

DESCRIPTION:

Oval sweets, 25mm long, 15mm wide, 10mm deep. Cowe's of Berwick pack their sweets in tins of 227g with a red and green design on the front. Colour: pale fawn with pink stripes. Flavour: mildly peppermint. Composition: sugar, water, glucose, mint and colouring.

HISTORY:

Berwick cockles take their name from the east-coast town of Berwick-upon-Tweed. They belong to a tradition of 'boilings' – a collective term for the boiled-sugar sweets popular in this region and north into Scotland. McNeill (1963) states they have been made in Berwick for nearly 200 years, suggesting a mid-eighteenth century origin but giving no evidence in support. Sweets of this general type, striped with red, have certainly been known in Britain since the early nineteenth century, when Stavely (1830) gave a recipe for Paradise Twist.

Wm. Cowe and Sons claims to be the originator of Berwick cockles. The sweets are packed in a tin which carries the legend, 'This tin contains Cowe's Genuine Original Celebrated Berwick Cockles; Delicious and Wholesome Sweetmeats. Entirely Different from Imitations; Purveyors to HRH the late Princess Mary Adelaide of Teck.' Similar confections are made by other companies in the Borders and south-eastern Scotland.

TECHNIQUE:

Cowe's recipe and method are trade secrets. A general method for producing this type of sweet requires a mixture of glucose and white and brown sugar made into a syrup and boiled to a temperature of about 145°C ('hard crack' in sugar-boilers' terms). This is stirred to induce graining (crystal formation by the sugar) and poured on a slab of marble or water-cooled steel. Peppermint flavouring is added. (Alternatively, the mass can be worked on a 'stretcher' – a machine which pulls the sugar mass, aerating it and lightening the colour.) A portion of the mixture is cut off from the main lump and coloured red; this is made into long narrow pieces and used to stripe the main batch. This is made into cockles either by spinning through a rock roller into long narrow pieces, which are then cut into short lengths, or putting through a drop roller which moulds the batch into small round shapes. After the sweets have cooled, they are allowed to mature for 7–10 days, during which time they reabsorb moisture and the texture softens.

REGION OF PRODUCTION:

BORDERS, BERWICK-UPON-TWEED (NORTHUMBERLAND).

Black Bullets

DESCRIPTION:

SPHERICAL SWEETS OF 20MM DIAMETER. WEIGHT: 6G. COLOUR: GOLDEN, TRANSLUCENT. FLAVOUR: MINT, BROWN SUGAR. COMPOSITION: SUGAR, GLUCOSE, OIL OF PEPPERMINT.

HISTORY:

In the dialect of the North-East, the word bullet indicates a hard, sugar sweet. It has had this meaning for at least 100 years and probably much longer. It derives from a diminutive of the French *boule*, used in English in the seventeenth century for small round objects made of various substances, for example, wax or wood. Apart from the fact that black bullets are small and round, there may be a more direct link with sugar boiling, as *petit boulé* (little ball or, more commonly now, soft ball) and *gros boulé* (large ball, or hard ball) are terms belonging to the special knowledge of the sugar confectioner. These are names for sugar solutions at 109–116°C and 120–126°C respectively.

Black bullets are in the general tradition of British high-boiled confectionery; the use of brown, unrefined sugar suggests an origin before the mid-nineteenth century when white sugar became cheap and widely available. There are several similar sweets made in other parts of the country, including Uncle Joe's Mint Balls (Lancashire). One brand, 'Jesmona', is a trademark belonging to Maxon's Ltd of Sheffield.

TECHNIQUE:

Black bullets are made from a syrup based on brown sugar, boiled to the 'hard crack' stage (145–150°C). The syrup is poured on a slab, and mint flavouring kneaded through it. It is formed into a rope, spun out and cut on a ball-spinning machine. The sweets break apart as they cool, giving smooth, round balls which are wrapped individually or packed in airtight tins.

REGION OF PRODUCTION:

North East England, Yorkshire.

*'We may live without friends; we may live without books
But civilized men cannot live without cooks.'*

Owen Meredith

Brown Ale (North East): Newcastle Brown Ale

DESCRIPTION:

Brown ales in the Newcastle style are drier and more alcoholic than others in England. Newcastle Brown is malty, dry, with nutty and fruity overtones. It is 4.7 per cent alcohol by volume.

HISTORY:

Brown ales are sweeter and less hoppy than bitters and pale ales, but a particular style has developed in the North-East – in between the sweet, old-fashioned browns still found in the South and the pale ales known in the Midlands.

The history of brewing in Newcastle-upon-Tyne goes back at least to the 1300s, when there are records of a brewers' guild. Scottish & Newcastle Breweries, the company which produces Newcastle Brown, was created by a merger of several smaller businesses. The ale was developed over a period of 3 years by a brewer named Colonel Porter and was launched in Newcastle in 1927. It is still brewed there.

TECHNIQUE:

This is a blend of 2 beers; one, the lighter, is marketed separately as Newcastle Amber. The other, stronger and darker, is just for blending. Both are made by the standard British brewing method. The malts used are pale ale and crystal (which is a slightly darker, fuller roast) and there is less emphasis on hops than in bitters. Newcastle Brown Ale has been awarded Protected Geographical Indication (PGI).

REGION OF PRODUCTION:

North East England.

Fentiman's Ginger Brew

DESCRIPTION:

A pale straw yellow; cloudy. It is sweet, with a strong ginger flavour and spicy, bitter herbal notes. There is a slight chilli 'kick', and mild carbonation. It is not more than 0.05 per cent alcohol by volume.

HISTORY:

The use of herbs and spices to flavour brewed drinks can be traced back to the late medieval period when long pepper, nutmeg and cinnamon were all recorded as being added to ale. The spices added flavour and probably had a preservative effect at a time when hops were unknown in Britain (Wilson, 1973). A tradition of flavoured ales continued well into the nineteenth century; one, known as 'Covent Garden Purl', was drunk as a hot, morning pick-me-up by Londoners.

Some sizeable brewers used ginger and liquorice in beer into the 1960s (Jackson, 1993).

During the 1800s, fermented ginger drinks with a low alcohol content became popular. An early recipe occurs under the name 'pop' in S.W. Stavely (1830); it is composed of water, lemons, cream of tartar, sugar and ginger, fermented for a few days. Fentiman's Ginger Brew, a cloudy drink made by a process of fermentation, but with a very low alcohol level, belongs to this tradition. The company originated before World War I, as 'Botanical Brewers', making soft drinks for a temperance and herbal tradition strong in the north of England. These drinks were eclipsed by fruit squashes and carbonated soft drinks but new interest has led to a revival of Fentiman's by a descendant of the original maker after a few years' absence from the market.

TECHNIQUE:

'Botanical brewing' means the drink is brewed from bruised roots and herbs. The bruised-root component, which gives the drink its character, comes from dried ginger root which is milled, boiled and mixed with essences derived from other herbs and sugar. The mixture is fermented with yeast until the alcohol content is 0.5 per cent, then pasteurized before bottling to guarantee that no more fermentation takes place. The alcohol content is strictly controlled so that this drink falls within the category of soft drinks. The drink is not strained and the ginger remains as a sediment; the bottle should be shaken before pouring.

Ingredients include fermented ginger root extract, carbonated water, sugar, glucose syrup, natural flavourings (ginger, capsicum, lemon, speedwell, juniper, yarrow), mono-potassium L tartrate, and citric acid. Only the one manufacturer makes Fentiman's Ginger Brew, but several others make a non-alcoholic carbonated ginger ale or strongly alcoholic ginger beer. These are based on conventional techniques, using malt sugar. Some are mixed with ginger essences, others use root ginger, added after the wort has been strained through the hop-back, and left immersed during fermentation.

REGION OF PRODUCTION:

NORTH EAST ENGLAND, NEWCASTLE-UPON-TYNE.

Mead: Lindisfarne Mead

DESCRIPTION:

LINDISFARNE MEAD IS PALE STRAW-GOLD, ITS FLAVOUR SWEET AND MILDLY SPICY WITH A HONEYED BOUQUET. IT IS 14.5 PER CENT ALCOHOL BY VOLUME.

HISTORY:

The word mead reaches back to the Indo-European root word for honey and exists in all Celtic and Teutonic languages of the British Isles. Fermented honey drinks have been made here from early times. The ancient geographer Strabo recorded that a honey drink was made in Ireland and other northern lands. It was one of the principal sources of alcoholic cheer in Anglo-Saxon England, referred to in heroic poems, chronicles and folk riddles. Mead was probably made by anyone who harvested honey; this included monasteries, whose monks kept bees to produce wax. In the simplest form, mead is a mixture of honey and water left to ferment under the action of wild yeasts. It existed in Britain in parallel with beer and ale: an Anglo-Saxon mead-seller is recorded in an early document, much like an alehouse-keeper. However, it was easier to make large quantities of beer than it was a honey-based drink. And wine, whether imported or home-produced, had a higher social standing.

A tradition of elaborate honey drinks mixed with ingredients such as apple or grape juice, and flavourings of herbs and spices, culminated in the seventeenth century, codified in many recipe collections. They were known as hydromel, melomel or metheglin. They were very dry and wine-like. The taste for such concoctions did not vanish immediately: Mrs Raffald (1769) gave a recipe for a fortified mead, mixed with sack (a sherry-like wine). However, these drinks were not produced commercially after the Middle Ages, being rather the preserve of the domestic still-room.

Imports of cheap sugar led to a decline in beekeeping and mead became a curiosity made by a few beekeepers for their own consumption. A revival of interest in traditional foods led to the experimental production of mead on a commercial scale in the late twentieth century. Lindisfarne Ltd was established in 1962 on Holy Island off the coast of Northumberland. The company emphasizes the historic connections of mead and the traditions of the Celtic monks who established the monastery.

TECHNIQUE:

This mead is based on an old English recipe evolved to suit modern tastes and preconcep-tions of honey drinks. A fermented grape base is mixed with honey, herbs and water.

REGION OF PRODUCTION:

HOLY ISLAND, NORTHUMBRIA.

MENU

The North

Isle of Man, North West England, North England, North East England

Address Book

Trade Associations and Interest Groups

Asparagus Growers Associaton www.british-asparagus.co.uk
Association of Master Bakers www.masterbakers.co.uk
Association of Scottish Shellfish Growers www.assg.co.uk
Bee Farmers Association www.beefarmers.co.uk
Biscuit, Cake, Chocolate and Confectionary Alliance www.bcca.org.
Bramley Apple Information Service www.bramleyapples.co.uk
Bee Keepers Association www.bbka.org.uk
British Carrot Growers Association www.bcga.info
British Cheese Board www.cheeseboard.co.uk
British Deer Farmers Association www.bdfa.co.uk
British Goose Producers Association www.goose.cc
British Herb Trade Association www.bhta.org.uk
British Pig Association www.britishpigs.co.uk
British Summer Fruits www.britishsummerfruits.co.uk
British Soft Drinks Association www.britishsoftdrinks.com
British Waterfowl Association www.waterfowl.org.uk
Brogdale Horticultural Trust www.brogdale.org
Campaign for Real Ale www.camra.org.uk

Carrot Growers Association www.bcga.info
Common Ground www.england-in-particular.info
Curry Club www.thecurryclub.org.uk
Dairy Trade Federation www.dairyuk.org
English Apples and Pears www.englishapplesandpears.co.uk
English Farm Cider Centre www.middlefarm.com
Food from Britain www.foodfrombritain.co.uk
Food and Drink Federation www.fdf.org.uk
Game Conservancy Trust www.gct.org.uk
Gin and Vodka Association of Great Britain
www.ginvodka.org
Guild of Q Butchers www.guildofqbutchers.com
Henry Doubleday Research Association
(organic gardening and food) www.gardenorganic.org.uk
Herb Society www.herbsociety.co.uk
Kentish Cobnuts Association
www.kentishcobnutsassciation.co.uk
Meat and Livestock Commission www.mlc.org.uk
National Fruit Collection www.webvalley.co.uk
National Association of Cider Makers www.cideruk.com
National Farmers Union www.nfuonline.com
National Federation of Women's Institutes www.womens-institute.co.uk
National Market Traders Federation www.nmtf.co.uk
National Sheep Association www.nationalsheep.org.uk
Quality Meat Scotland www.qmscotland.co.uk
Rare Breeds Survival Trust www.rbst.org.uk
Sausage Appreciation Society www.sausagefans.com
Scotch Malt Whisky Society www.smws.com
Scottish Association of Master Bakers www.samb.co.uk
Scottish Association of Meat Wholesalers
www.scottish-meat-wholesalers.org.uk
Scottish Crop Research Institute www.scri.sari.ac.uk

Scottish Federation of Meat Traders Association www.sfmta.co.uk
Scottish Quality Salmon www.scottishsalmon.co.uk
Sea Fish Industry Authority www.seafish.org.uk
Seasoning and Spice Association (UK) www.seasoningandspice.org.uk
Shellfish Association of Great Britain www.shellfish.org.uk
Soil Association www.soilassociation.org
South-West of England Cider Makers Association http://tinyurl.com/pylmg
Specialist Cheesemakers Association www.specialistcheesemakers.co.uk
Taste of Shropshire www.shropshiretourism.info/food-and-drink/
Taste of the West www.tasteofthewest.co.uk
Taste of Wales Ltd www.wela.co.uk
Tastes of Anglia Ltd www.tastesofanglia.com
Three Counties Cider and Perry Association www.thethreecountiesciderandperryassociation.co.uk
Traditional Farm Fresh Turkey Association www.golden-promise.co.uk
UK Tea Council www.teacouncil.co.uk
United Kingdom Vineyards Association www.englishwineproducers.com
Watercress Growers Association www.watercress.co.uk
Wine and Spirit Trade Association www.wsta.co.uk

Producers, Suppliers and Particular Interest Groups

This is by no means an exhaustive list, but this list will point readers wishing to sample a taste of Britain in the right direction. Where possible, a website is given. For smaller organizations or individuals without a functioning website, a postal address is given.

The address book echoes the structure of the text, organized into categories that roughly reflect the natural order of a visit to market: fruit and vegetables, dairy, fishmonger, butchery, bakery, confectioners, drinks and condiments.

Fruit

Damson

The Mason's Arms at Cartmel Fell www.strawberrybank.com

Forced rhubarb

The National Rhubarb Collection, Harlow Carr Gardens, Harrogate, North Yorkshire HG3 1QB.

Ribston Pippin

Ampleforth Abbey Orchards, Ampleforth Abbey, Ampleforth, Yorkshire YO6 4HA.

Vegetables

Dock pudding

Mytholmroyd Community Centre, Elphaborough, Mytholmroyd, Hebden Bridge HX7 5DY.

Dairy Produce

Cheese

Cheshire cheese

Appleby's www.applebysofhawstone.co.uk

H. S. Bourne www.hsbourne.co.uk

Cotherstone cheese

Joan Cross, Quarry House, Marwood, Barnard Castle, County Durham DL12 9Q

Coverdale cheese

N. Reaks, Fountains Dairy Products, Kirkby Malzeard, Ripon, North Yorkshire HG4 3QD.

Ribblesdale cheese
I. and C. Hill, Ashes Farm, Horton in Ribblesdale, Settle, North Yorkshire, BD24 0JB.
Swaledale cheese
The Swaledale Cheese Company www.swaledalecheese.co.uk
Wensleydale cheese
S. Stirke, Fortmayne Farm Dairy, Newton-le-Willows, Bedale, Yorkshire DL8 1SL.
Wensleydale Dairy Products www.wensleydale.co.uk
Fountains Dairy Products Ltd, Kirkby Malzeard, Ripon, North Yorkshire HG4 3QD.

Fish & Seafood

Kipper (Craster)
L. Robson and Sons www.kipper.co.uk
Swallow Fish www.swallowfish.co.uk
Kipper (Manx)
George Devereaux and Son www.isleofmankippers.com
John Curtis www.manxkippers.com
Kipper (Whitby)
Fortunes, 22 Henrietta Street, Whitby, Yorkshire YO22 4DW.
R.J. Noble, 113, Church Street, Whitby,Yorkshire YO21.
Morecambe Bay shrimp
Martin Boyce, NW and N Wales Sea Fisheries Committee www.nwnwsfc.org
Potted shrimp
James Baxter and Son, Thornton Road, Morecambe, Lancashire LA4 5PB.
Scallop
Dr A.R. Brand, Port Erin Marine Laboratory, University of Liverpool, Port Erin, Isle of Man.

Meat

Sheep
Herdwick sheep
Herdwick Sheep Breeders Association www.herdwick-sheep.com
Agnus Farm Meats, Low Wool Oaks, Penrith, Cumbria CA11 9SZ.
Manx Loghtan sheep
Manx Loaghtan Breeders Group
http://vts2.dnsalias.com/manxbreeders/html/000index3.html

Pigs

Middle White pig

M. Squire The Middle White Breeder's Club, Benson Lodge, 50 Old Slade Lane, Iver, Buckinghamshire SL0 9DR.

Meat Products

Black pudding

Morris Pork Butchers, 120 Market Street, Farnworth, Bolton BL4 9AE.

Cumberland air-dried ham

Richard Woodall www.richardwoodall.com
Sillfield Farm www.sillfield.co.uk

Cumberland sausages

Richard Woodall www.richardwoodall.com
J. Cranston, Cranston's Butchers, Brampton, Cumbria.

Denby Dale pie

The Denby Dale Pie Company www.denbydalepie.co.uk
York ham
Harris-Leeming Bar, Leases Road, Leeming Bar, Northallerton, DL7 9AW.
George Scott, 81 Low Petergate, York, YO1 7HY.
Radford Butchers, 81 Coach Road, Sleights, Whitby YO21 5EH.

Breads

Borrowdale tea bread

The Village Bakery www.village-bakery.com

Glasgow rolls

Morton's Rolls, 2 Allardyce Road, Glasgow G15 6RX.

Stotty cakes

Gregg's Bakers www.greggs.co.uk

Griddle-breads, biscuits & Puddings

Grasmere gingerbread

The Gingerbread Gingerbread Shop
www.grasmeregingerbread.co.uk

Muffin

Betty's & Taylors of Harrogate www.bettysandtaylors.com

Suet cake
Southam's of Haworth Ltd, Fairfax Street, Haworth, Keighley, West Yorkshire.
Whitby gingerbread
Elizabeth Botham and Sons www.botham.co.uk

Cakes & Pies

Fat rascals
Betty's Café Tea Rooms www.bettys.co.uk
Kendal pepper cake
J. R. Birkett and Sons Ltd, Hutton Hall Bakery, Benson Row, Penrith, Cumbria CA11 7YN.
Ripon spice cakes
Davill's Patisserie, 24 Westgate, Ripon, North Yorkshire HG4 2BQ.
Seed cakes
Meg Rivers Cakes www.megrivers.com
Wilfra tart
Davill's Patisserie, 24 Westgate, Ripon, North Yorkshire, HG4 2BQ.
Whitby lemon buns
Elizabeth Botham and Sons www.botham.co.uk
Ainsley's of Leeds www.ainsleys.co.uk
Yorkshire mint pasty
Southams Bakers, Fairfax Street, Haworth, Keighley, West Yorkshire BD22 8JA.

Confectionery

Berwick cockles
Gibbs, Fort Matilda, Greenock PA16 7SZ.
James Ross and Son, Pentland Industrial Estate, Loanhead, Midlothian, Scotland EH20 9QR.
Black bullets
Maxons Ltd www.maxons.co.uk
Coltsfoot rock
Stockley Sweets Ltd www.stockleys-sweets.co.uk
Fisherman's Friends
Lofthouse of Fleetwood Ltd www.fishermansfriend.com
Kendal mint cake
Romney's Kendal Mint Cake www.kendal.mintcake.co.uk
J.E. Wilson and Sons www.funchocs.com
D. Quiggin and Son www.quiggins.co.uk

Lily of the valley creams
J. Fairbank, Bonnet's, 38–40 Huntriss Row, Scarborough YO1 1ES.
Pontefract cakes
Dunhill's www.haribo.com/planet/uk/info/frameset.php
Monkhill Confectionery www.cadbury.co.uk

Aromatics & Condiments

Raspberry vinegar
Seldom Seen Farm www.seldomseenfarm.co.uk
Les Fines Herbes, 8 St Mary's Hill, Stamford, Lincolnshire PE9 2DP.
Womersley Famous Fruit and Herb Delicacies
www.womersleyfinefoods.co.uk
Spring Farm Shop, The Moor, Trowell, Nottinghamshire NG9 3PQ

Beverages

Bitter beer (Tadcaster)
Samuel Smith's Old Brewery
www.merchantduvin.com/pages/5_breweries/samsmith.html
The Black Sheep Brewery www.blacksheepbrewery.com
Black beer
J.E. Mather and Sons Ltd, Barchester Winery, Silver Royd Hill, Leeds LS12 4JL.
Matthew Clark Gaymer Ltd www.matthewclark.co.uk
Brown ale
Scottish and Newcastle Breweries www.scottish-newcastle.com
Dandelion and burdock
Ben Shaw Ltd www.benshaws.com
A.G. Barr plc www.agbarr.co.uk
Fitzpatrick's Herbal Health Shop www.fitzpatricks1890.co.uk
Fentiman's ginger brew
Fentiman's www.botanically-brewed-soft-drinks.co.uk
Mead
St Aidan's Winery www.lindisfarne-mead.co.uk
Oatmeal stout
Samuel Smith's Old Brewery
www.merchantduvin.com/pages/5_breweries/samsmith.html
Old ale (Yorkshire)
T.& R. Theakston Ltd www.theakston.co.uk

Porter
Elgood and Sons Ltd www.elgoods-brewery.co.uk
Young's www.youngs.co.uk
Tizer
A.G. Barr plc www.agbarr.co.uk
Vimto
J.N. Nichols plc www.nicholsplc.co.uk
Fitzpatrick's Herbal Health Shop www.fitzpatricks1890.co.uk

PGOs and PGIs

Britain and continental Europe possess an enormous range of wonderful food. When a product's reputation extends beyond national borders, however, it can find itself in competition with products using the same name and passing themselves off as genuine. This unfair competition discourages producers and misleads consumers, and for this reason the European Union in 1992 created systems known as Protected Designation of Origin and Protected Geographical Indication to promote and protect regionally important food products. A Protected Designation of Origin (PDO) describes a food that is produced, processed and prepared in a given geographical area, using a recognised skill. A Protected Geographical Indication (PGI) demonstrates a geographical link between a foodstuff and a specific region in at least one of the stages of production, processing or preparation.
For more information, visit
http://ec.europa.eu/agriculture/qual/en/uk_en.htm

Bibliography

Unless otherwise indicated, the place of publication is London and the country of publication is the United Kingdom.

Beeton, Isabella (1861), *Beeton's Book of Household Management*, facsimile ed. 1982, Chancellor Press.

Bostwick, D. (1988), 'The Denby Dale Pies', Folk Life.

Boyd, Lizzie (1976), *British Cookery*, Croom Helm, Bromley.

Bradley, Martha (1756), *The British Housewife*, facsimile ed. 1997-8, Prospect Books, Totnes.

Brears, P. (1984), *The Gentlewoman's Kitchen*, Wakefeld Historical Publications, Wakefeld.

——— (1987), *Traditional Food in Yorkshire*, John Donald, Edinburgh.

Brown, Lynda (1987), 'Elder, a good udder to dinner', Petits Propos Culinaires 26.

Cassell's (1896), *Cassell's Dictionary of Cookery* (first ed. c. 1875).

Cutting, C.L. (1955), *Fish Saving, A History of Fish Processing from Ancient to Modern Times*, Hill.

Clark, Colette, ed. (1960), *Home at Grasmere*, Penguin Books.

Dallas, E.S. (1877), *Kettner's Book of The Table*, facsimile ed.1968, Centaur Press.

David, Elizabeth (1968), *English Potted Meats and Fish Pastes*, reprinted in *An Omelette and a Glass of Wine*, (1984), Robert Hale.

——— (1970), *Spices, Salt and Aromatics in the English Kitchen*, Penguin Books.

——— (1977), *English Bread and Yeast Cookery*, Allen Lane.

——— (1992), 'Anglo-American Tomato Ketchup', Petits Propos Culinaires 40.

Dawson, Thomas (1596), *The Good Housewifes Jewell*, ed. Maggie Black, 1996, Southover Press, Lewes.

Dunkling, L. (1992), *The Guinness Drinking Companion*, Guinness Publishing, Enfeld.

Dyson, John (1977), *Business in Great Waters*, Angus and Robertson.

Eales, M. (1733), *Receipts*, facsimile ed. 1985, Prospect Books.

Finney, Thomas B. (1915), *Handy Guide for Pork Butchers*, Finney & Co, Manchester.

Glasse, Hannah (1747), *The Art of Cookery Made Plain and Easy*, facsimile 1983, Prospect Books.

——— (1772), *The Compleat Confectioner.*

Hall, S.J.G. and Clutton-Brock, J. (1989), *Two Hundred Years of British Farm Livestock*, British Museum.

Hallam, J. (1979), *The Gingerbread Ladies.*

Hartley, Dorothy (1954), *Food in England*, Macdonald and Janes.

Hieatt, Constance A. (1986), *An Ordinance of Pottage*, Prospect Books.

Hogan, W. (1978), *The Complete Book of Bacon*, Northwood Publications.

ICA Test Kitchen (1971), *Swedish Cooking*, Vasteras, Sweden.

Jackson, Michael (1989), *Malt Whisky Companion*, Dorling Kindersley.

——— (1993), *Michael Jackson's Beer Companion*, Mitchell Beazley.

Kirkland, J. (1907), *The Modern Baker, Confectioner and Caterer*, Gresham Publishing Company.

Lutes, Della (1938), *The Country Kitchen*, 1985 ed., Bell & Hyman.

Mabey, David (1978), *In Search of Food, traditional eating and drinking in Britain*, Macdonald and Jane's.

Mackenzie, Compton (1954), *Echoes*, Chatto & Windus.

MacLean, Donald (n.d.), *Potato Varieties, a Fact sheet on Special Properties.*

McNeill, F.M. (1929), *The Scots Kitchen*, Blackie, Glasgow.
——— (1946), *Recipes from Scotland*, Albyn, Edinburgh.
——— (1956), *The Scots Cellar*, Lochar, Moffat (1992).
——— (1963), *The Scots Kitchen* (2nd ed.), Blackie, Glasgow.
Man, R. and Weir, R. (1988), *The Compleat Mustard*, Constable.
Marshall, Mrs A.B. (1887), *Mrs A.B. Marshall's Cookery Book*, 1st ed. (n.d.)
Marshall, M.W. (1987), *Fishing, the coastal tradition*, BT Batsford Ltd.
Mayhew, Henry (1861), *London Labour and the London Poor*.
Mitchell, W.R. March (1986), 'A Taste of Swaledale Cheese', The Dalesman.
Montagu, F. (1938), *Gleanings in Craven*.
Nicholson and Burn, (1777), *The History of Cumberland and Westmoreland*.
Nott, J. (1726), *Cook's and Confectioner's Dictionary*, facsimile ed. 1980, Lawrence Rivington.
Plat, Sir Hugh (1602), *Delightes for Ladies*, modern ed. 1948, Crosby Lockwood.
Pollard, Helen (1991), 'Lancashire's Heritage', *Traditional Food East and West of the Pennines*, ed. C.A. Wilson, Edinburgh University Press.
Poulson, J. (1978), *Lakeland Recipes Old and New*, Countryside Publications, Chorley.
Race, M. (1990), *The Story of Blackpool Rock*, Blackpool.
Raffald, E. (1769), *The Experienced English Housekeeper*, facsimile of 1782 ed. 1970, E&W Books.
Rance, Patrick (1982), *The Great British Cheese Book*, Macmillan.
Roach, F.A. (1985), *Cultivated Fruits of Britain*, Basil Blackwell, Oxford.
Roberts, Robert (1971), *The Classic Slum*, (Penguin Books ed., 1973).
Samuel, S. (1860), (ed.), *The Pig*, by William Youatt.
Schofield, E.M. (1973), 'Working Class Food and Cooking in 1900', Folk Life, vol. 13.
Shipperbottom, R.(1995), 'The Decline of Tripe', *Disappearing Foods,* Oxford Symposium on Food and Cookery, ed. Harlan Walker, Prospect Books, Totnes.
Smith, C. (1951), 'My Lady's Caprice', *The Critic*, October.
Smith, Eliza (1758), *The Compleat Housewife*, first published 1727, facsimile of the 16th ed., 1983, Arlon House Publishing, Kings Langley.
Smith, J. (1989), *Fairs, Feasts and Frolics, customs and traditions in Yorkshire*, Smith Settle, Otley.
Spicer, D.G. (1949), *From an English Oven*, The Women's Press, New York, USA.
Spurling, Hilary (1987), *Elinor Fettiplace's Receipt Book*, Penguin Books.
Stavely, S.W. (1830) *The Whole New Art of Confectionary*, Derby.
Stead, Jennifer (1991), 'Prodigal Frugality', *Traditional Food East and West of the Pennines*, ed. C.A. Wilson, Edinburgh University Press.
Stocker, D. (1988), *Potted Tales, Recollections and views of Morecambe Bay Fishermen*, Lancaster City Museums, Lancaster.
Tibbott, Minwel (1976), *Welsh Fare*, The National Museum of Wales, Cardiff.
——— (1986) 'Liberality and Hospitality, food as communication in Wales', Folk Life, vol. 24.
White, Florence (1932), *Good Things in England*, Jonathan Cape.
Wilson, C. Anne (1973), *Food and Drink in Britain*, Constable.
——— (1985), 'I'll to Thee a Simnel Bring', *Petits Propos Culinaires* 19.
——— (1985), *The Book of Marmalade*, Constable.
——— (1991), (ed.), B*anquetting Stuffe*, Edinburgh University Press.
Wondrausch, Mary (1995), 'Potted Char', *Disappearing Foods, Oxford Symposium on Food and Cookery*, ed. Harlan Walker, Prospect Books, Totnes.
Wright, Joseph (1896–1905), *The English Dialect Dictionary*, Henry Frowde.

Acknowledgements

Isle of Man, North West England, North England, North East England

From Eccles Cake to Hawkshead Wig

A Celebration of Northern Food

Particular thanks to the following chefs, authors and journalists who generously contributed pieces to the book:

Bruce Poole (p.16-7), Simon Rimmer (p.57), Rose Prince (p118-9).

The following people have kindly given the compilers information about particular foods and trades. This book could not have been completed without their assistance.

T. Alty, Preston, Lancashire; C. Bench, Thistleton, Rutland; E. Biltoft, Ripon, North Yorkshire; J. Botham, Whitby, Yorkshire; A.R. Brand, Port Erin, Isle of Man; P. Brears, Leeds, West Yorkshire; P. Canipa, Douglas, Isle of Man; A. Churchward, Severn-Trent River Authority, Tewkesbury; K. Davill, Ripon, North Yorkshire; A. Elliott, Ambleside, Cumbria; J. Elmhurst, Barnsley, Yorkshire; W. Fortune, Whitby, Yorkshire; S. Fudge, Sherborne, Dorset; L. Garrad, Douglas, Isle of Man; P. Graham, Hawkshead, Cumbria; T. Grayson, Leeds, West Yorkshire; M. Hackett, Lindisfarne, Northumberland; M. Hall, Southam's Bakery, Haworth, West Yorkshire; P. Holmes, Upper Denby, West Yorkshire; B. Keen, Peel, Isle of Man; P. Lawson, Stockley's, Accrington, Lancashire; C. Margrave, Harrogate, North Yorkshire; K. Mason, Ilkley, West Yorkshire; M. Muggeridge, Runcorn, Cheshire; L. Patterson, Gosforth, Tyne & Wear; J.R. Pitchfork, Sheffeld; H. Pollard, Kendal, Cumbria; D. Reed, Richmond, Yorkshire; J.A. Rivis and staff, Helmsley, North Yorkshire; C. Robinson, Grange-over-Sands, Cumbria; A. Robson, Craster, Northumberland; S. Saunders, Blackpool, Lancashire; F.W. Shepherd, Newcastle and District Allotment Society, Newcastle upon Tyne; The late R. Shipperbottom, Stockport, Cheshire; S. Smith, Leeming Bar, North Yorkshire; J. Stead, Leeds, Yorkshire; M. Stewart, Sherborne, Dorset; S. Stirke, Bedale, North Yorkshire; D. Thomasson, Dorchester; J. Trehane, Wimborne, Dorset; P. van Reale, Pontefract, West Yorkshire; E. Vigeon, Manchester; B. Waddington, Rawtenstall, Lancashire; S. Wickham, Mytholmroyd, West Yorkshire; A. Winter, University of Liverpool; N. Wood, Sherborne, Dorset; R. Woodall, Waberthwaite, Cumbria; B. Wordsworth, Barnoldswick, Lancashire; P. Zissler, Darlington, County Durham.